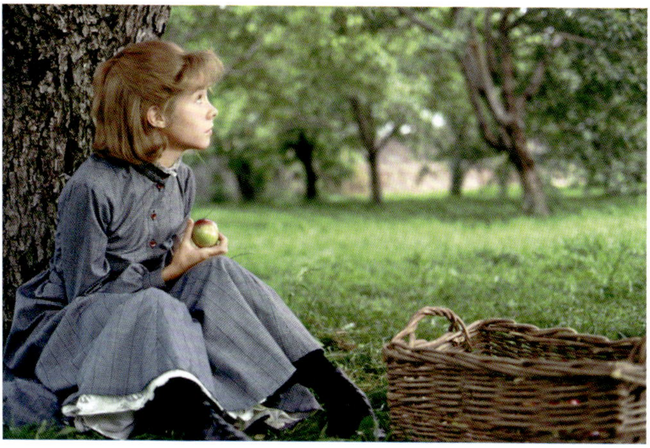

To the legions of enthusiastic fans and homemakers who have *peppered me* with questions about the kind of prop food that was served on the Green Gables kitchen set during filming.

Kevin Sullivan

Library and Archives Canada Cataloguing in Publication

Sullivan, Kevin, 1955 May 28-

    Cooking with Anne of Green Gables : recipes from Edwardian kitchens : from the producers of Anne of Green Gables and Road to Avonlea / Kevin Sullivan.

ISBN-13: 978-0-9736803-5-5
ISBN-10: 0-9736803-5-0

    1. Cookery, Canadian--Prince Edward Island style.
2. Literary cookbooks. 3. Shirley, Anne (Fictitious character)
I. Title.

TX715.6.S85 2005   641.59717   C2005-906868-X

Copyright 2005 by Sullivan Entertainment Inc.
Published in 2005 by Davenport Press, Toronto, Canada.

Printed and bound in China.

All rights reserved. No part of this book may be reproduced in any form or by any electronic or mechanical means, including information storage and retrieval systems, without the prior written permission from the publisher, except for reviewers who may quote brief passages.

Front Cover : Anne Shirley (Megan Follows) *is responsible for a spectacular autumn picnic in "Anne of Green Gables - The Sequel".*
Back Cover: Anne (Megan Follows) *is invited to tea by Miss Josephine Barry* (Charmian King).
Title Page: Anne (Megan Follows) *waits in the orchard at Green Gables farm..*

Cooking With
Anne of Green Gables

Recipes from
Edwardian Kitchens

From the Producers of

Anne of Green Gables

and

Road to Avonlea

DAVENPORT PRESS, PUBLISHERS
WWW.SULLIVANMOVIES.COM

Table of Contents

Foreword by Kevin Sullivan 04

Introduction 05

Cooking in the early 1900's 06

Turn-of-the Century Etiquette 08

Planning an Authentic Anne of Green Gables meal 11

Appetizers 12

Breads 18

Soups 30

Seafood 36

Main course 44

Vegetables 52

Salads 58

Dessert 66

Drinks 76

Preserves 82

Victorian Parlour Games 90

Foreword by Kevin Sullivan

In 1984 I drove along numerous rural back roads looking for a landscape that could capture the idyllic maritime farming community of turn-of-the-century PEI in my television adaptation of "*Anne of Green Gables*". Ironically I found the location that became the production's signature about 15 minutes from Leaksdale, Ontario, and the town where L.M. Montgomery and her family lived for a decade after they'd moved away from PEI.

Out of the corner of my car window I caught sight of a wave of rolling fields, crested with pines into which was nestled a charming, rambling whitewashed farmhouse that looked remarkably as if the ocean was located just on the other side of the hill. I adapted the farm building and barns and successfully shot them for all of the mythical looking reverses of the *"Green Gables"* Farm.

The atmosphere of any film is established through a myriad of details from production design, costume, props to set decoration. The source of inspiration for making films often has as much to do with the environment where a performance takes place as it does with a dramatic premise. Choosing a setting to entertain in can be as imaginative an experience as selecting a movie location. Mood and surroundings are as important for a special occasion as a menu. Through recipes and anecdotes on Victorian and Edwardian lifestyle this book is intended to allow an audience to evoke the mood of *"Green Gables"* in the same manner as a production crew would prepare to bring a movie dining table to life.

Entertaining can be a wonderful form of self-expression. Whether the event is whimsical or stately, as the company moves through all of the courses, I hope that the environment conjured up on these pages raises the experience above the ordinary.

Introduction

At the beginning of the 1900s when *Anne* would have lived, a woman's place was in the home and she was expected to find satisfaction in running a well-ordered household. Her typical day would have included cooking, cleaning, laundry, child care, tending the sick, splitting the kindling, stoking the fires and hopefully having some time left for reading, sewing, visiting neighbours and resting. While headstrong *Anne Shirley* certainly doesn't fit the mold of a typical Edwardian lady there is no doubt that she would have been a skilled cook, if not out of love then out of necessity. Anne always enjoyed the experience of creating a special dish. Just remember how excited she was when she finally had the chance to act as hostess when she invited Diana to tea. While the results were less than perfect, it was an experience that she never forgot. That is really what cooking is all about at the end of the day. Beside the obvious purpose of providing nourishment, each recipe is a story waiting to be told. Stories that were written long ago and passed on from mother to daughter. Through re-creating these recipes here on these pages, one can take a step back in time, to smell, taste and feel what it must have been like to cook in P.E.I. at the turn-of-the-century, how it must have been to cook like *"Anne of Green Gables"*.

Sullivan rehearsing on set with Megan Follows

Cooking in the Early 1900s

Before you begin trying the recipes inspired by Anne, you first need to appreciate what it must have been like cooking in Prince Edward Island in the early 1900s. Only the rich could afford iceboxes or running water so that most households, like the Cuthberts, would have stored their butter and cream either in a dugout in the kitchen floor, the icehouse or down in the well. They did their dishes using the backyard pump. Farm families worked from dawn to dark, raising cows and chickens, growing their fruits and vegetables, churning butter and baking bread. They went to town by horse and buggy on Saturday to buy oatmeal, sugar, molasses, beans and prunes, perhaps some sweets for the kids and a bolt of cloth for a new dress. They often lived miles from their nearest neighbors, so visitors were always welcomed and offered something to eat. The first thing said was, "Will you stay for supper?" There was always an extra place available at the table and nothing was wasted. Soup was made from the bone and then the marrow of the bone was eaten. Mass-produced goods like ketchup, tea, cheese and meats were just beginning to become available with the introduction of the first refrigerator rail cars.

The White Sands Hotel from "Road to Avonlea"

Sarah Polley and Jackie Burroughs serve tea in "Road to Avonlea"

Most cooks however depended strictly on their regional ingredients. In the coastal province of P.E.I this meant an abundance of seafood and potatoes concocted in an unending number of inventive ways.

Cooking truly underscored every social occasion. Tarts, cones, and small cakes were prepared when the Ladies Aid met or the preacher came to visit. Muffins, raisin cookies and hefty spice cakes were carried to the men in the field. Food was brought to schoolhouse dances and all kinds of "bees" from sewing to barn-raising, as well as shivarees at the homes of newlyweds. Box Socials involved home-packed fancy lunches in decorated boxes which were auctioned off to the highest bidder (thus igniting many a romance). In cities, the rich often dined in extravagant style. Fourteen course banquets that began with oysters, progressed through fish and meat dishes, and ended with three desserts plus an assortment of liqueurs.

Living on a farm, Anne would have dined fairly modestly, but she always tried to make the occasion special. The easiest way to accomplish something special is to present a meal elegantly, to show your guests how much you care about them. The following are recommendations from the time that Anne lived, on how a hostess should set her table and behave.

Turn-of-the-Century Etiquette

TABLE SETTING

An attractive display of the food makes it even more appetizing. It denotes that this dining occasion is special and encourages children to behave respectfully. Aside from esthetics though, the primary goal of table setting should be for the convenience and comfort of the dining guests. Therefore the following rules are merely guidelines and should not be followed slavishly.

TABLE LINENS

All linens must be immaculate and should be chosen to harmonize with the room and furniture. The tablecloth should have a skirt of at least 12 inches. Allow 24 inches of space across for each setting. Place mats should be at least 12 x 8 inches and napkins should be 18 inches square. Place mats should be in line with the table and directly across from one another unless there are an odd number of guests. If using lace napkins, it is practical to couple them with linen napkins. The napkin is placed to the left of the fork for an informal dinner or on the plate for a formal dinner.

DINNERWARE

There are four principle types of dinnerware: bone china, semi-porcelain, porcelain or earthenware. Bone china is the finest of them all and should be accompanied with dainty silverware and fine crystal to create an overall harmonious look. Porcelain and earthenware are porous and one must be careful of long-term stains or discoloration when using them. They also tend to be heavier than china. Plates should be placed one inch from the edge of the table. The butter plate is placed in the top left corner of each place mat.

GLASSWARE

The quality of the glasses should match the selected dinnerware. Therefore the heavy cut glass goblets always works best with porcelain rather than china. A water glass should be placed at the tip of the knife.

SILVERWARE

Set the table with all the pieces that will be needed and no more. They should be placed in a straight line, one inch from the edge of the table and should be placed in order of use from the outside in, towards the plate. Fork is on the left unless a knife is not being used and spoons are outside of the knife. Knife blades should be facing the plate edge. Butter knife is on the butter plate horizontal to the guest. Silverware for the food dishes should be placed beside the food dishes and never in them.

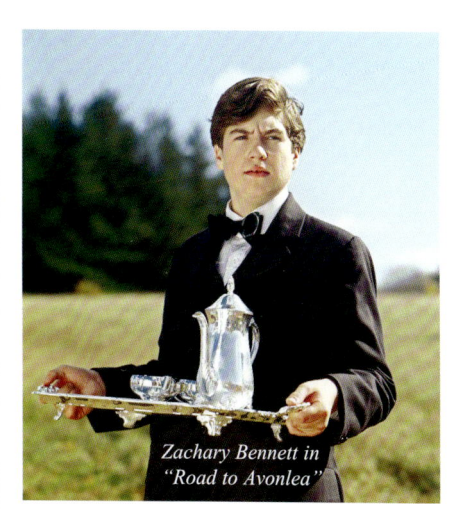

Zachary Bennett in "Road to Avonlea"

DECORATIONS

Table decorations provide a point of interest on the table. While flowers are the most classic and perhaps the most beautiful choice of adornment, there are many other creative means of decoration. A bowl of fruit, figurines, potted plants, basket of seashells or colorful stones all display imagination. Candles should only be used if they are to be lit. All table decoration should not interfere with the guests' sightline across the table. Allow one set of salt and pepper for each pair of people.

GREETING THE GUESTS

Guests should arrive ten to five minutes before the dinner hour and be dressed in attire befitting the occasion. The hostess should greet each guest as they arrive and see that the meal is served at the appointed time.

SEATING

The hostess directs the seating; ladies are at the right of the host and gentlemen on the left. The host should offer his arm and escort the female guest of honour to her seat. Placecards are generally used if more than eight people are to be seated. They should be simple and placed on the napkin.

MENU ETIQUETTE

Bread and water should be placed on the table just before the guests are seated. Cold appetizers may be placed on the table in advance. It is essential to hire help for serving the meal, especially for formal dinners. The hostess should remain at the table during the meal and only supervise the waitress. If it is a less formal occasion the food can be served *English style* where the host carves the meat and the hostess serves the vegetables, passing the plates to the left. If the tea and coffee are served in the living room then the hostess may pour and pass the cups. The host is responsible for managing the dinner conversation and steering it away from heated or controversial subjects. Guests should converse with other guests in the spirit of the occasion. Guests should remain two hours after the dinner is finished unless bridge, music or theatre have been suggested as part of the invitation. The guest of honour should be the first to leave unless it is a group of intimate friends; in which case some may stay while others depart. Upon departing, the guests should thank the hostess and ought to follow up with a note of written thanks within a few days.

The White Sands Hotel from "Road to Avonlea"

Planning an Authentic Anne of Green Gables Meal

With some sense of turn-of-the-century guidelines it is an easy and intriguing adventure to plan an authentic *Green Gables* dinner.

This recipe book is divided into courses that should begin with Appetizers, followed by Breads, Soups, Fish, Main Dish (of meat, chicken or pork) with Vegetables, Salad, Dessert and after dinner Drinks. Select at least one item from each category. Keep in mind which ingredients are seasonal, since Anne would have had limited access to imported vegetables or fruits. Also balance the flavours of your selections so that if you start with a fishy appetizer follow it with a sourdough bread and perhaps a spicy soup. Each course should be different but complementary. Most important, plan the meal ultimately with the pleasure of your guests in mind. A meal should always be designed as a form of entertainment.

The Strawberry Social from "Anne of Green Gables"

Appetizers

Appetizers are like meeting someone for the first time. They could be exotic or familiar but hopefully they intrigue you and make you want to discover more. If there was an Anne appetizer you would expect a fiery dip with crisp crudites which would set the stage for a classy but adventurous meal, followed by a sweet dessert to finish. Bon appetit!

Hot Crab Almond Dip

1 cup cream cheese
1 can crab meat, drained
1 ½ cups blanched almonds
2 tablespoons chopped onion
1 tablespoon milk
½ teaspoon horseradish
¼ teaspoon salt
¼ teaspoon pepper

Mix well, place in an 8 inch pie plate. Cover with blanched, halved almonds. Bake at 375F for 15 minutes. Serve with Melba toast, crackers, rusks, etc.

Croute Bernard

1 tablespoon butter
2 slices bacon, finely chopped
1 medium onion, finely chopped
6 mushrooms, finely chopped
1 cup grated Swiss cheese
1 cup grated strong Canadian Cheddar cheese
½ cup (4 oz) dry white wine
1 whole egg
8 slices toast

Melt butter in a saucepan. Add bacon, onion and mushrooms and cook for 5 minutes. Add wine and reduce over medium heat for 3 minutes. Remove from heat and let cool. Then add cheese and egg and mix well with a wooden spoon. Salt and pepper to taste. Spoon onto toast. Sprinkle with paprika. Bake in a 375F oven 5 or 6 minutes or until heated through and golden brown. You can cut the crust off the bread and make large rounds, if you wish, or buy round bread. For a cocktail party, you can cut the bread any size you wish. This toast can be prepared well in advance and frozen. Just pop toasts in the oven when you are ready to serve.

Cheese Straws

*¼ cup grated old Canadian Cheddar cheese
sprinkle of paprika*

Preheat oven to 450F. Prepare half of a Flaky Pastry (see recipe under *Desserts*). Roll out into a rectangle on a lightly floured surface. Cover half of dough with cheese. Sprinkle with paprika. Fold over and pinch edges together. Fold over again, pinching edges. Roll out about ¼ inch thick. Cut in 4 inch x ½ inch strips. Twist and place on ungreased baking sheet. Bake in a 450F oven for 8 to 10 minutes, or until crisp and golden brown.

Solomon Grundy

*2 salt herrings
1 cup vinegar (sufficient to cover herring)
1 tablespoon granulated sugar
a pinch of pepper
1 onion, sliced
4-6 pickled red pepper strips*

Thoroughly clean and remove the skin from the herring. Fillet and cut in two 2-inch pieces. Soak in cold water for 5 hours, changing water frequently. Drain. Heat the vinegar. Remove from heat and stir in the granulated sugar and pepper. Allow to cool. Pour over herring and add the sliced onion, letting it stand for a few hours. Serve squares of marinated herring on slices of raw onion set on a cracker or on toast. Garnish with pickled red pepper strips.

Corn Fritters

*1 ⅓ cups all-purpose flour
1 ½ teaspoons baking powder
½ teaspoon salt
2 ½ cups creamed corn
1 egg, beaten*

Preheat oil in deep fryer to 375F. Blend together dry ingredients, then add corn and egg. Drop by spoonfuls into fryer. Fry for 5 minutes, turning to ensure even browning. Drain on absorbent paper. Keep warm in a 300F oven until all are cooked. Makes 18 fritters.

Baddock Scotch Eggs

3 hard-cooked eggs
½ pound skinless sausages or sausage meat
1 egg, slightly beaten
1 cup bread crumbs
¼ cup chopped parsley

Preheat deep fat to 375F. Cool and shell the hard-cooked eggs. Mash the sausages/sausage meat, then shape around eggs, covering completely. Dip in the slightly beaten egg and roll in bread crumbs. Fry in deep fat for 3 to 4 minutes, or until golden brown. Cut in half and sprinkle with parsley. Serve hot or cold. Makes 3 servings.

Caulcannon

2 white potatoes
1 turnip
1 white cabbage
3 parsnips
1 onion
1 cup butter
1 teaspoon salt
a dash of pepper

Wash and then cook together the potatoes, turnip, cabbage, parsnips and onion. Then put through potato ricer. Mix well in a saucepan with butter, salt and pepper. Heat thoroughly.

Salmon Caviar Spread

213 g. (7.5 oz) tin sockeye salmon, drained
250 g. pkg cream cheese, softened
1 tbsp. lemon juice from a fresh lemon
2 tbsp. grated onions
1 ½ tsp. horseradish

Flake salmon, discarding skin and bones. Combine cream cheese, lemon juice, onion and horseradish. Add salmon and mix again. Serve with wheat crackers (225 g. box).

Salmon Paté

1 pound red salmon
1 cup cream cheese
1 tablespoon lemon juice
2 teaspoons horseradish
1 teaspoon grated raw onion
¼ teaspoon salt
¼ teaspoon Worcestershire sauce
¼ teaspoon Tabasco
6 tablespoons chopped pecans or walnuts
2 tablespoons chopped parsley

Blend cheese in blender or processor, then add all remaining ingredients, except nuts and parsley. Mix well. Refrigerate overnight, then shape into a ball and roll in parsley and nuts. Serve with crackers.

Chicken Liver Paté

2 tablespoons chopped onion
6 tablespoons butter
1 pound chicken livers
1 ½ cups consomme or bouillon
2 tablespoons dry sherry
¼ teaspoon paprika
1 teaspoon dry mustard
¼ teaspoon ground cloves
½ teaspoon ginger
⅛ teaspoon Tabasco
½ teaspoon salt
1 minced clove of garlic
3 teaspoons brandy
1 package unflavored gelatin

Saute onions in skillet with butter until tender but not brown. Add chicken livers and cook over medium heat for 10 minutes. Stir in consomme, sherry, paprika, mustard, cloves, ginger, tabasco, salt and garlic and cook 5 minutes. Blend chicken liver with electric mixer and then set aside. Put consomme in saucepan, sprinkle gelatin over it. Heat and stir until gelatin is dissolved. Arrange some olive or mushrooms slices in bottom of loaf pan. Pour ¼ of this mixture over olives. Refrigerate 15 minutes. Mix remainder of gelatin with chicken livers and then pour over olive base. Refrigerate 6 hours.

Marinated Goat Cheese

1 pound goat cheese (chevre)
½ cup black olives, chopped
1 tsp. dried rosemary
1 tsp. black peppercorns
¼ onion, chopped
2 cloves garlic, minced
Olive oil

Crumble cheese. Add olives, rosemary, peppercorns, onions and garlic. Cover with olive oil. Refrigerate. Serve with whole wheat crackers. Keep refrigerated for an extended period of time.

Bruschetta

Fresh tomatoes or 1 can stewed
1 tsp. basil
¼ cup olive oil
½ tsp. garlic
1 small onion, finely chopped
⅓ cup green pepper

Mix above and spoon over slightly toasted English muffins. Heat in 375F oven for a few minutes. Serve immediately.

Colleen Dewhurst, Patricia Hamilton and Megan Follows in "Anne of Green Gables"

Breads

Bread is the unsung hero of any meal. You couldn't have a sandwich without bread anymore than Anne could have become the fine woman she did without Marilla. It was Marilla's firm but gentle guidance that kept putting Anne back on the path that her pride and temper sometimes led her away from. It was Marilla that told Anne to follow her dreams with the promise that she would always be able to return home to Green Gables. She provided Anne with the bread of life, a staple of unconditional love that she could rely on forever.

Salmon Loaf

2 cups canned salmon
1 cup mashed cooked potatoes
½ cup milk
1½ cups crushed cracker crumbs
2 eggs
2 tablespoons lemon juice
1 tablespoon butter
½ teaspoon salt
¼ teaspoon pepper

Combine the ingredients into a paste and then pack them into a greased bowl or fish shaped mould. Cover with wax paper and foil. Tie tightly. Steam for 1½ hours. Serve hot, with lemon or egg sauce, or serve cold, with mayonnaise.

Shediac Brown Bread

1 cup all-purpose flour
1½ teaspoons salt
1 teaspoon baking powder
1 teaspoon baking soda
1 cup cornmeal
1 cup whole wheat flour
2 tablespoons brown sugar
¾ cup molasses
1¼ cups water
2 tablespoons shortening, melted

Thoroughly grease two 3½ cup (28-oz.) baking tins. Sift together flour, salt, baking powder and baking soda. Stir in cornmeal, flour and sugar. Beat the molasses, water and shortening together with a fork. Add liquids to the dry ingredients and stir only until combined (batter will be lumpy). Fill prepared tins ⅔ full. Cover with wax paper and foil and tie securely. Steam for 2 hours on a rack in a pan with water to half the height of the tins. Unmold. Slice and serve warm or cold, but spread with butter. Makes 2 or 3 loaves.
Preparing Raisin Brown Bread: Stir in 1 cup raisins before filling tins.

Sourdough Bread

1 teaspoon granulated sugar
3½ cups lukewarm water (100F)
1 envelope active dry yeast
1 tablespoon salt
1 tablespoon sugar
9½ to 10 cups all-purpose flour
1 cup milk
¼ cup granulated sugar
2 tablespoons shortening

Preheat oven to 400F. In a large bowl dissolve granulated sugar in ½ cup lukewarm water. Over this, sprinkle yeast. Let stand for 10 minutes, then stir briskly with a fork. Stir in salt, sugar, 3 cups flour and the remaining water. Cover. Let stand for 3 days, stirring down batter daily. On third day scald milk. Stir in granulated sugar and shortening. Cool to lukewarm. Blend in 3 cups yeast mixture. To remainder add 2 cups lukewarm water and 2 cups all-purpose flour. Let stand at room temperature one day, then pour into glass jar, seal and refrigerate. Use for next batch of bread. Beat in 3 cups all-purpose flour. Add another 3½ to 4 cups all-purpose flour. Work in last of flour with a rotating motion of the hand. Turn dough out on a lightly floured surface and knead 8 to 10 minutes. Shape into a smooth ball and place in a greased bowl, rotating dough to grease surface. Cover, and let rise until doubled (about 1¼ hours). Turn out on lightly floured board and knead until smooth. Divide in three. Roll out each portion and shape into loaves. Place in greased 8½ x 4½-inch loaf pans. Grease tops and let rise again until doubled (about 45 minutes). Bake in 400F oven for 30 to 55 minutes. Makes 3 loaves.

100% Whole Wheat Bread

2 ¾ cups milk
⅓ cup molasses
4 teaspoons salt
2 teaspoons sugar
1 cup lukewarm water (100F)
2 envelopes active dry yeast
8 to 9 cups whole wheat flour

Preheat oven to 350F. Scald milk. Pour into a large bowl and stir in molasses and salt. Cool to lukewarm. Meanwhile dissolve sugar in water. Over this, sprinkle yeast. Let stand for 10 minutes. Then stir briskly with a fork. Add softened yeast to lukewarm mixture. Stir. Beat in 4 cups whole wheat flour. Work in last of flour with a rotating motion of the hand. Turn dough out on a lightly floured surface and knead 8 to 10 minutes. Shape into a smooth ball and place in a greased bowl, rotating dough to grease the surface. Cover, and let rise until doubled (about 2 hours). Punch down, and shape into 3 loaves. Place in greased 8 ½ x 4 ½-inch loaf pans. Grease tops and let rise again until doubled (about 1 hour). Bake in 350F oven for 40 to 45 minutes. Makes 3 loaves.

Trapper's Bread

1½ cups raisins
1½ cups currants
2¾ cups hot water
1 cup lightly packed brown sugar
1 tablespoon salt
1 cup butter
⅔ to 1 cup molasses
2 teaspoons sugar
1 cup lukewarm water (100F)
2 envelopes active dry yeast
12 cups all-purpose flour

Preheat oven to 375F. Cover raisins and currants with boiling water, allow them to plump and then drain. In a large bowl combine 2 ¼ cups of hot water with brown sugar, salt, butter and molasses. Sir until butter melts. Cool to lukewarm. Meanwhile, dissolve sugar in 1 cup of lukewarm water. Sprinkle yeast on top of this sugar water and let stand for 10 minutes. After 10 minutes, stir briskly with a fork. Combine softened yeast mixture with lukewarm molasses water. Stir in 6 cups all-purpose flour. Mix plumped fruit with the remaining flour. Work in last of flour mixture with a rotating motion of the hand. Turn dough out on a lightly floured surface. Cover with damp cloth and let rise until doubled (about 2 hours). Punch down and shape into 4 loaves. Place in greased 8 ½ x 4 ½-inch loaf pans, cover, and let rise again until doubled (about 1 hour). Bake in preheated 375F oven for 1 hour. Brush tops with butter while still hot. Makes 4 loaves.

French Bread

½ cup milk
¼ cup water
1 tablespoon granulated sugar
2 teaspoons salt
2 tablespoons shortening
1 teaspoon granulated sugar
¼ teaspoon ginger
½ cup water, lukewarm (100F)
1 envelope active dry yeast
4½ cups all-purpose flour
1 egg white
2 tablespoons water

Scald together milk and ¼ cup of water. Pour into a large bowl and add tablespoon of sugar, salt, and shortening. Stir until shortening melts. Cool mixture to lukewarm. Meanwhile, dissolve teaspoon of sugar and ginger into the ½ cup lukewarm water. Over this, sprinkle dry yeast. Let stand for 10 minutes. Then stir briskly with a fork. Add softened yeast to lukewarm milk mixture. Stir. Beat in 2 ½ cups all-purpose flour. Add the rest of the flour. Work in with a rotating motion of the hand. Turn dough out on a lightly floured surface and knead for 8 to 10 minutes. Shape into a smooth ball and place in a lightly greased bowl, rotating dough to grease surface. Cover with a damp cloth and let rise in a warm place until doubled (about 1½ hours). Punch down the dough and turn out on a lightly floured surface. Divide dough into three parts, forming each portion into a smooth ball. Cover and let rise for 15 minutes. Knead each portion and shape into a narrow 12 loaf. Place well apart on a greased baking sheet. With scissors, slash tops diagonally. Cover with a damp cloth and let rise in a warm place until doubled (in unheated oven with a pan of boiling water underneath improves crustiness). Bake in preheated 400F oven for 15 minutes, then reduce heat to 350F for 25 minutes. Brush with egg white mixed with 2 tablespoons water twice during baking. Makes 3 loaves.

Mary's Polish Bread

1 teaspoon sugar
¼ cup water, lukewarm (100F)
1 envelope active dry yeast
2 cups water, lukewarm
1 cup all-purpose flour
1 cup rolled oats
1 tablespoon salt
3 cups graham flour
2 tablespoons Caraway seeds

Dissolve sugar into ¼ cup lukewarm water, sprinkle yeast packet overtop. Let stand for 10 minutes. Then stir briskly with a fork. Stir softened yeast into 2 cups lukewarm water. Beat in flour, rolled oats, salt. Add graham flour and caraway seeds. Work in last of flour with a rotating motion of the hand. Turn dough out on a lightly floured surface and knead 8 to 10 minutes. Shape into 2 loaves, cover with damp cloth and let rise until doubled. Bake in preheated 375F oven for 55 to 65 minutes. Makes 2 loaves.

Oatmeal Brown Bread

1 cup rolled oats
2 teaspoons salt
1 tablespoon butter
2 cups boiling water
1 teaspoon sugar
½ cup lukewarm water (100F)
1 envelope active dry yeast
½ cup molasses
1 cup whole wheat flour
5 cups all purpose flour

Preheat oven to 375F. Combine in a large bowl: rolled oats, salt and butter. Pour boiling water over top. Stir until butter melts. Cool to lukewarm. Meanwhile, dissolve sugar in lukewarm water. Sprinkle yeast packet over top. Let stand for 10 minutes. Then stir briskly with a fork. Add softened yeast to lukewarm water mixture, together with molasses. Beat in whole wheat flour, then 2 cups all-purpose flour. Add remainder of flour, working it in with a rotating motion of the hand. Turn dough out on a lightly floured surface and knead 8 to 10 minutes. Shape into a smooth ball and place in a greased bowl, rotating dough to grease surface. Cover and let rise until doubled (about 1½ hours). Punch down and shape into 3 loaves. Place in 8 ½ x 4 ½ inch loaf pans, grease tops and let rise again until doubled. Bake in preheated 375F oven for 60 to 65 minutes. Makes 3 loaves.

Sweet Dough

2 cups milk, scalded and cooled to lukewarm (100F)
1 teaspoon sugar
½ cup lukewarm water
1 envelope active dry yeast
9 ½ cups all-purpose flour
1 cup granulated sugar
½ teaspoon salt
½ cup butter, melted
1 tablespoon grated lemon rind
4 whole eggs

Dissolve 1 teaspoon sugar in ½ cup lukewarm water. Sprinkle active dry yeast packet and let stand for 10 minutes. Stir briskly with a fork. Add softened yeast to lukewarm milk. Stir. Beat in 3 cups all-purpose flour. Cover bowl. Let stand in warm place until light and full of bubbles (about 1 hour). Stir in 1 cup sugar, ½ teaspoon salt, ½ cup melted butter, and the grated lemon rind. Beat 4 whole eggs with a fork, and stir into batter. Add 2 cups all-purpose flour. Beat vigorously. Add another 4 cups flour. Work the mixture in with a rotating motion of the hand. Turn dough out on a lightly floured surface and knead 8 to 10 minutes. Shape into a smooth ball and place in a greased bowl, rotating dough to grease surface. Cover and let rise until doubled (about 1 ½ hours).

Icing Sugar Glaze

¾ cup sifted icing sugar
1 tablespoon milk
¼ teaspoon almond flavouring

Mix together icing sugar, milk, almond flavoring, and spread on hot yeast breads.

Hot Cross Buns

¾ cup milk
½ cup granulated sugar
1 teaspoon salt
¼ cup butter
1 teaspoon sugar
½ cup lukewarm water
1 envelope active dry yeast
1 egg, beaten
1 egg yolk
1 teaspoon cinnamon
½ teaspoon cloves
¼ teaspoon nutmeg
4 cups all-purpose flour
½ cup raisins or currants
1 slightly beaten egg white
1 tablespoon water

Scald milk and pour into a large bowl and add ½ teaspoon sugar, salt, and butter. Stir until butter melts. Cool until lukewarm. Meanwhile, dissolve a teaspoon of sugar in lukewarm water (100F). Over this, sprinkle dry active yeast. Let stand for 10 minutes. Then stir briskly with a fork. Add softened yeast to lukewarm milk mixture together with beaten egg, yolk, cinnamon, cloves, nutmeg. Beat in 2 cups flour. Add another 2 cups of additional flour while working dough in a rotating motion. Turn dough out on a lightly floured surface and knead for 8 to 10 minutes. Knead in raisins or currants. Shape into a smooth ball and place in a lightly greased bowl, rotating dough to grease surface. Cover with a damp cloth and let rise in a warm place until doubled (about 1½ hours). Punch down the dough and arrange 2 inches apart on a greased baking sheet. Cover with a damp cloth and let rise in a warm place until doubled (about 45 minutes). Combine slightly beaten egg white and 1 teaspoon water and brush on buns. Slash top of bun in the form of a cross. Bake in a preheated oven for 15 to 18 minutes. Drizzle with icing sugar glaze (see page 24). Serve halved and toasted. Makes 18 to 24 buns.

Maple Syrup Buns

1 cup milk
½ cup granulated sugar
2 teaspoons salt
¾ cup shortening
1 cup mashed cooked potatoes (2 medium potatoes)
2 eggs, beaten
1 tablespoon cinnamon
1 teaspoon sugar
½ cup water, lukewarm (100F)
1 envelope active dry yeast
1 ½ cups raisins
5 cups all-purpose flour
½ cup maple syrup
1 tablespoon granulated sugar

Scald milk and pour into a large bowl. Add sugar, salt, shortening, mashed potatoes, 1 cup flour, eggs, and cinnamon. Stir until shortening melts. Cool to lukewarm. Meanwhile, dissolve 1 teaspoon sugar in lukewarm water and sprinkle active dry yeast over top. Let stand for 10 minutes. Then stir briskly with a fork. Add softened yeast to lukewarm milk mixture (mixture will be liquidy). Stir, then cover with wax paper and a damp cloth. Let stand in a warm place for 2 hours. Cover raisins with boiling water, allow to plump, then drain. Stir raisins into batter along with 2 cups all-purpose flour. Add 2 additional cups all-purpose flour. Work in last cup of flour with a rotating motion of the hand. Turn dough out on a lightly floured surface and knead 8 to 10 minutes. Shape into a smooth ball and place in a greased bowl, rotating dough to grease surface. Cover and let rise until doubled (about 2 hours). Roll dough out ½ inch thick and cut with a 2 inch cookie cutter. Place on greased baking sheet. Cover and let rise 15 minutes. Bake in preheated 400F oven for 15 to 18 minutes, or until golden brown. Boil maple syrup and sugar together until it forms a thread (230F on a candy thermometer). Drizzle on buns while they are still hot. Makes about 4 dozen buns.

Chelsea Buns

½ cup butter
2 ⅓ cups brown sugar, lightly packed
1 ½ tablespoons corn syrup
⅔ cup coarsely chopped pecans

3 tablespoons soft butter
1 teaspoon cinnamon
¾ cup seedless raisins

Preheat oven to 375F. Melt ½ cup butter in 13 x 9 inch cake pan. Stir in 1 ⅓ cups lightly packed brown sugar and ½ tablespoon corn syrup. Blend until smooth. Sprinkle with pecans. Allow to cool. Roll out slightly more than one third of the dough on a lightly floured surface into a rectangle 24 x 9 inches. Spread with 3 tablespoons soft butter. Sprinkle with a mixture of remaining brown sugar, cinnamon and raisins. Distribute as evenly as possible over top. Roll up like a jelly roll and cut into pieces about 1 inch long. Arrange closely together in a prepared pan, cut side up. Cover and let rise until doubled (about 1¼ hours). Bake in preheated 375F oven for 30 to 35 minutes, or until golden brown. Turn pan upside down on rack immediately. Allow syrup to run over rolls for several minutes before removing the pan. Makes about 24 buns.

Scones

2 cups flour
1 teaspoon salt
4 teaspoons baking powder
5 tablespoons white sugar
½ cup margarine
2 eggs
½ cup milk
¼ cup currants (washed)

Put flour, salt, baking powder and sugar in a bowl. Add margarine and mix with wire pastry blender. Mix eggs and milk separately in a bowl. Add to dry ingredients. Add currants. Roll out ½ inch thick on floured board. Cut in wedges. Bake at 350F for 15 minutes.

Tea Biscuits

2¼ cups all-purpose flour
4 teaspoons baking powder
1 teaspoon salt
½ cup shortening
1 cup milk

Preheat oven to 450F. Sift or blend together flour, baking powder and salt. With a pastry blender or two knives, cut in shortening until crumbly. Stir in milk. Mix lightly with a fork to make a soft, slightly sticky dough. Turn dough out on a lightly floured surface and knead gently 8 to 10 times. Roll out or pat down until 1 inch thick. Cut with floured 1 ¾-inch cookie cutter or floured glass tumbler. Bake on ungreased baking sheet in 450F oven for 12 to 15 minutes, or until light golden brown. Serve hot or cold, with butter and jam. Makes 18 to 20 biscuits.

Salt Pork Buns

1 cup finely chopped salt pork
3¾ cups all-purpose flour
2 tablespoons baking powder
½ teaspoon salt
¼ cup butter
½ cup molasses
1½ cups water

Preheat oven to 425F. Fry pork until crisp. Drain well. Sift or blend together flour, baking powder and salt. With a pastry blender or two knives, cut butter in, until crumbly. Stir in cooked salt pork (locally called *scrunchions*). Combine and add molasses and water. Stir with a fork to make a soft, slightly sticky dough. Turn dough out on a lightly floured surface and knead gently 8 to 10 times. Roll out or pat to ½ inch thick. Cut with floured 3-inch wide cookie cutter. Place 1 inch apart on ungreased baking sheet and bake in 425F oven for 12 to 15 minutes, or until brown. Serve hot, with butter. Makes 30 biscuits.

Perfect Popovers

1 cup all-purpose flour
½ teaspoon salt
2 eggs
1 cup milk
4 teaspoons beef drippings
1 tablespoon butter

Preheat oven to 450F. Pour ½ teaspoon beef drippings in each of 8 medium-sized muffin cups. Keep warm in oven. Blend together flour and salt. Beat eggs, milk and butter together with mixer or rotary beater. Add flour mixture and beat 2 minutes. Pour into prepared pans. Bake in 450F oven for 20 minutes and serve immediately. If reheating - slit each popover once to allow steam to escape. Turn oven off and leave popover in another 20 minutes.

Soda Bread

2 cup all purpose flour
1 tsp. baking powder
1 tsp. baking soda
½ tsp. salt
2 tbsp. margarine
1 cup buttermilk
½ cup of raisins

Combine flour, soda, salt, raisins and baking powder. Rub margarine in with fingertips. Add buttermilk and stir with a fork to make soft dough. Turn out on floured board and knead lightly. Shape into a ball and flatten slightly. With a sharp knife, make a cross on top. Bake at 400F for 15 minutes. Reduce heat to 350F and bake 30 minutes.

Megan Follows and Colleen Dewhurst in "Anne of Green Gables - The Sequel"

Soups

Soup has long been considered a comfort food; a tonic for the sick and even the broken hearted. Anne had more than her share of troubles despite the fact that she brought many of them on herself. Here in Marilla's garden, Anne nurses a bleeding heart for Gilbert Blythe, even though it was Anne who pushed Gilbert away and turned down his marriage proposal. How much soup Marilla must have prepared, to solve Anne's troubled spirit!

P.E.I. Potato Soup

3 to 4 medium potatoes, quartered
3 cups boiling water
1 teaspoon salt
2 cups undiluted evaporated milk
1 tablespoon grated onion
3 tablespoons butter
a pinch of pepper
½ cup grated cheese (Mozzarella recommended)

Together, cook the potatoes, boiling water and salt in a covered saucepan for 25 minutes, or until tender. (Part chicken or beef stock may be used instead of water.) Drain and reserve the liquid and press potatoes through a sieve. Combine evaporated milk, onion, butter and pepper in a large saucepan. Heat, but do not boil. Stir in sieved potatoes. Reheat and add water if necessary. Season to taste. Stir in grated cheese. Heat until cheese melts. Serve garnished with chopped parsley. Makes 6 servings.

Old-Fashioned Split Pea Soup

2 cups split green peas
12 cups cold water
4 whole cloves
1 bay leaf
1 ham-bone, fat removed
1 cup finely chopped onion
1 cup finely diced carrots
2 beef bouillon cubes

Pick over and wash the split green peas. In a large kettle combine the peas with the water. Bring to a boil, cover and remove from the heat. Let stand 1 hour. Wrapping the cloves and bay leaf loosely in cheesecloth, add to the kettle with ham-bone, onion, celery, carrots and beef bouillon cubes. Bring to a boil. Cover and simmer gently, 1½ to 2 hours, or until peas are soft. Remove ham bone and spice bag. Puree soup in a blender or press through a sieve, and reheat in soup kettle with finely diced ham from bone. Season to taste, using approximately 1 tablespoon salt and ¼ teaspoon pepper. Amount of salt will vary depending on the type of ham. Makes 8 to 10 servings.

Pumpkin Soup

2 pounds pumpkin
1 onion, large, finely chopped
2 tomatoes, sliced
2 teaspoons chives, chopped
sprig parsley
1 cup chicken stock
½ cup single cream or milk
a pinch of salt, to taste
2 dashes liquid hot pepper sauce
dash paprika
dash nutmeg

Cut the pumpkin into big pieces and cook in boiling, salted water for 15 minutes. Drain. Scoop the flesh from the skin. Put the pumpkin and all the other vegetables, half the chives and the parsley with the chicken stock in a saucepan. Bring to boil, lower heat and simmer for approximately 35 minutes with the lid on the pan. Allow to cool slightly, mix in blender with cream or milk. Season with salt, paprika, nutmeg and hot pepper sauce. Serve hot or cold.

Cheese Soup

2 onions, chopped
3 tablespoons butter
2 tablespoons all-purpose flour
1 ¼ cups condensed beef bouillon
3 cups milk
3 cups grated processed Cheddar cheese

Fry onions in butter until transparent. Stir in the flour then gradually add the bouillon. Cook this mixture until thickened, stirring constantly. Add in the milk and simmer for 15 minutes. Remove from heat and strain. Discard remnants and keep liquid at a simmer. Stir in grated cheese until smooth. Serves 4.

Scottish Broth

⅓ cup pearl barley
3 pounds stewing lamb
8 cups cold water
2 teaspoons salt
¼ teaspoon pepper
1 cup chopped onion
1 crushed bay leaf
2 whole cloves
½ cup diced turnip
½ cup diced celery
½ cup diced carrots
½ cup diced potato

Soak the barley for a minimum of 2 hours in sufficient water to cover it. Trim all the fat from the lamb and cut into two-inch pieces. In a large saucepan combine the meat, bones, cold water, salt and pepper and bring to a boil. Stir in ½ cup of the chopped onion. Loosely wrap the bay leaf and cloves in cheesecloth and place in the saucepan. Allow to simmer covered for 45 minutes. Remove the bones and spice bag and allow to cool, then skim the fat from the broth. Add the drained barley into the broth and bring to a boil. Cover and simmer for 45 minutes. Stir in the rest of the chopped onion, turnip, celery, carrots and potato and bring to a boil. Simmer for 30 minutes or until vegetables are tender. Season to taste with salt and pepper. Serves 6.

Cold Borscht

2 cups diced raw beets
1 green onion (chopped)
2 cups sour cream
pinch chopped fresh dill
pinch salt

Wash the beets and then chop into small pieces. Stir the chopped beets and onion into the sour cream. Divide the mixture and using a blender, puree one half at a time. Season to taste with dill and salt. Garnish with more dill. Serves 4.

Clam & Celery Bisque

1 large can baby clams
2 teaspoons butter
2 tablespoons chopped onion
2 tablespoons flour
½ teaspoon salt
1 can celery soup
1 can tomato soup
1 pinch thyme
2 pinches mace
2 cups skim milk

Drain clams; reserve juice. Rinse clams under cold running water; drain. Strain juice through cheesecloth. Saute onion in butter for 2 minutes. Remove from heat, stir in flour, clam juice and salt. Cook until thick. Stir in all the remaining ingredients except for the milk and clams. Bring to a boil; add milk and clams. Reheat thoroughly, without boiling. Serve piping hot and add sherry to each serving. Serves 4-6.

Fish Chowder

1 pound fillets, fresh or smoked
2 tablespoons butter
1 medium onion, sliced
½ cup diced celery
2 cups diced potatoes
½ cup sliced carrots
2 cups boiling water
1 teaspoon salt
a pinch of pepper
2 cups milk

Cut fillets into bite-sized pieces. In a large saucepan, sautee the onion and celery in the butter until tender. Add the potatoes, carrots, boiling water, salt and pepper. Cover and simmer for 10 minutes, or until vegetables are tender. Add fish and cook for 10 minutes longer. Add milk. Reheat, but do not boil. Makes 6 servings.

Clam Chowder

¼ pound salt pork, diced
1 onion, finely diced
3 or 4 potatoes, diced
1½ cups boiling water
1 cup canned tomatoes (if desired)
2 cans clams (10 ounces each)
3 ½ cups milk (approx.)
½ cup cream (18% m.g.)
1 teaspoon salt
1 teaspoon celery salt
a pinch of pepper
2 teaspoons butter

Fry the pork in a large saucepan. Drain and reserve drippings. Cook the onion in the pork drippings until transparent but not browned. Add the potatoes, boiling water, and canned tomatoes. Bring to a boil and reduce heat. Cover, and cook for 10 minutes, or until potatoes are just tender. Drain and reserve liquid from the clams. Measure clam liquid and add sufficient milk to make 4 cups. Add to cooked potatoes and heat slowly just to boiling point. Stir in drained clams and crisp pork together with cream, salt, celery salt, pepper and butter. Reheat just to boiling point and season to taste. Serve garnished with paprika or parsley. If desired, substitute salt pork with 4 slices side bacon; and 2 cans of clam with 1-pint fresh clams in liquor. Makes 8 to 10 servings.

Vichysoisse

1 - 10 ½ oz. can cream of potato soup
1 - 10 ½ oz. can cream of chicken soup
1 soup can milk
1 cup cream (18% m.g.)

Put first 3 ingredients in blender; blend till smooth. Add cream. Blend again to combine. Chill for 3 or 4 hours. Service with chopped chives.

Seafood

Being located on beautiful Prince Edward Island, the ocean and the bounty of fare it offered would have played an important role in the lives of those in Avonlea. Gilbert was most certainly an accomplished fisherman and his best prize was pulled from Barry's pond. While role-playing as the Lily Maid of Camelot, Anne became stranded under a bridge when the boat she was floating in sank. Thankfully Gilbert came along and although she put up a proud fight, he managed to to land her in his dory and get her safely back to shore. What a catch!

Scalloped Oysters

1 ¼ cups shucked (shelled) oysters
1¼ cups coarse cracker crumbs
½ cup melted butter
½ teaspoon Worcestershire sauce
¼ teaspoon salt
a pinch of pepper
¼ cup milk

Preheat oven to 350F. Place the oysters alternately with cracker crumbs in a thoroughly greased casserole. Combine melted butter, Worcestershire sauce, salt and pepper together. Pour liquid over the oysters and cover with a layer of crumbs. Pour milk over top. Bake in 350F oven for 30 minutes. Makes 2 to 3 servings.

French Fried Scallops

1 pound scallops
¼ cup all-purpose flour
1 teaspoon salt
pinch pepper
1 egg
2 tablespoons cold water
¾ cup fine dry bread crumbs

Heat deep fat fryer to 375F. Wipe the scallops with a damp cloth and cut if necessary. Roll the scallops in a mixture of flour, salt and pepper, then dip in a mixture of egg and water. Roll in dry bread crumbs. Fry in preheated deep fat for about 3 to 4 minutes, or until golden brown. Serve with tartar sauce. Makes 3 to 4 servings.

Fish Cakes

1 pound fresh cod or haddock
1 cup cooked mashed potatoes
1 small chopped onion
2 tablespoons melted butter
1 egg, beaten
3 to 4 tablespoons chopped parsley
a dash of salt
a pinch of pepper

Cover the fresh cod or haddock with cold water and bring slowly to a simmer. Drain and flake the fish. Combine drained flaked fish with mashed potatoes, onion, butter, egg, chopped parsley, salt and pepper. Shape into cakes (if necessary use a little flour to hold them together). If desired, cakes may be coated with ¼ cup fine dry breadcrumbs. Pan fry in hot fat until crisp and brown. Turn and brown other side. May be served with tomato sauce or heated chili sauce. Makes 4 to 6 servings.

Soused Herring or Mackerel

2 pounds fresh herring or mackerel
1 cup vinegar
½ cup water
1 teaspoon salt
1 tablespoon mixed pickling spices
2 thin slices of onion

Preheat oven to 350F. Fillet and skin the herring or mackerel. Cut into serving pieces. Place the fish in a bake dish and add the vinegar, water, salt, pickling spices and onion. Cover and bake in 350F oven for 15 minutes. Allow to cool in liquid. Drain before serving. Makes 3 to 4 servings.

Broiled Lobster

4 lobsters (1 pound)
LOTS of melted butter, vinegar, salt and pepper!

Plunge the 4 lobsters into boiling water for about 5 minutes. Remove from the water. Split lengthwise and clean. Remove the dark vein that runs through the body at the center. Cut off membrane. Discard sac or "lady" behind the head. Open as flat as possible. Lay shell side down on grill, or shell side up on broiler pan. Broil or barbecue using medium heat, for 15 minutes longer. Serve with melted butter, vinegar, salt and pepper.

Maddock Finnan Haddie

1 smoked haddock
1 tablespoon butter
¾ cup milk
1 tablespoon cornstarch

Skin and cut the haddock into pieces. Lay the pieces in a heavy pan and dot with butter. Cover pan and steam for 5 minutes. Add the cornstarch to the milk and stir until completely dissolved. Pour milk over fish and bring to a boil. Boil for 1 minute. Serve with sauce poured over fish.

Stuffed Halibut Steaks

¼ cup butter
¼ cup chopped onion
¼ cup diced celery
½ teaspoon salt
¼ teaspoon seasoning (savory, thyme, tarragon, sage, mint, poultry seasoning etc.)
2 cups soft bread crumbs
1 tomato, chopped
2 halibut steaks (about 1 lb. each)

Preheat oven to 450F. Grease baking dish. In a frying pan, melt the butter and then fry the chopped onion and diced celery for about 15 minutes. Add salt and seasoning. Stir in the bread crumbs and then add a tomato. Spread the stuffing between the halibut steaks. Place in a prepared baking dish. Brush with melted butter. Measure the total thickness of the steaks and stuffing. Bake in 450F oven, allowing 10 minutes per inch thickness for fresh fish, 20 minutes per inch thickness for frozen fish. Makes 4 to 6 servings.

Hugger-In-Buff

1 pound salt cod
4 medium potatoes
¼ pound fat salt pork, diced
2 medium onions, sliced
2 tablespoons vinegar
¼ cup milk

Freshen the salt cod by covering completely with water and soaking overnight. Cut in serving portions. Peel the 4 potatoes and cut into eighths. Place the cod and potatoes in a saucepan. Cover with boiling water and simmer for about 20 minutes, or until potatoes are tender. Drain and place on a warm platter. While the fish and potatoes are cooking, fry the diced salt pork until it becomes crispy. Remove the pork scraps from the pan. Place onions in the pan and cook, returning the pork once the onions have become tender. Add in vinegar and milk. Bring the liquid to a boil and pour over potatoes and cod. Makes 4 servings.

Cod au Gratin

1 pound cod fillets
1½ cups milk
3 tablespoons butter, melted
4 tablespoons flour
½ teaspoon salt
a pinch of pepper
2 tablespoons grated cheese

Preheat oven to 350F. Grease 3 individual casseroles. Simmer the cod fillets in milk (taking care not to boil the milk) until the fillets flake easily. Drain, reserving the liquid. (If necessary, add cold milk to make 1½ cups of liquid). Flake cod into prepared casseroles. Combine the butter, flour, salt and pepper in a saucepan and cook over medium heat gradually stirring in the reserved liquid. Cook, stirring constantly, until thickened. Add ½ cup sauce to each casserole. Top each with 2 tablespoons grated cheese. Place casseroles in a shallow pan containing about ¼ inch of water. Bake in 350F oven for 15 to 20 minutes, or until piping hot and cheese is melted. Makes 3 servings.

Fish Rolls

1 pound fresh fillets (cod, haddock or sole)
3 tablespoons soft butter
2½ cups coarse soft bread crumbs
1 tablespoon finely chopped onion
1 tablespoon chopped parsley
1 teaspoon salt
a pinch of pepper
1 egg, slightly beaten
2 tablespoons flour
2 tablespoons shortening
1 can (10 ounces) condensed cream of mushroom soup

Preheat oven to 350F. Spread flat the fish fillets (if very thick, split into thin, lengthwise slices). Combine together 1½ cups bread crumbs, 2 tablespoons butter, chopped onion, chopped parsley, 1 teaspoon salt, a pinch of pepper and 1 slightly beaten egg. Spread stuffing on fillets. Roll up like a jelly roll and secure with toothpicks. Coat rolls with a mixture of flour and salt and pepper. In a frying pan, brown in the shortening. Arrange rolls in a shallow baking dish and spread with cream of mushroom soup. Sprinkle with a mixture of 1 tablespoon butter, 1 cup bread crumbs and a pinch of salt. Bake in 350F oven for 40 minutes, or until fish flakes easily with a fork. Makes 4 servings.

Clam Pie

2 cans clams
1/4 pound side bacon, diced
5 medium potatoes
2 medium onions (thinly sliced)
1/2 teaspoon salt
1/2 teaspoon pepper
2 cups liquid (clam liquor plus water)

Preheat oven 325F. Grease a 13 inch x 9 inch baking pan. Strain the clams reserving the liquid. Wash the clams well. Pan fry the diced side bacon until crispy. Peel and thinly slice the potatoes. Arrange half of the potatoes in a prepared pan with half of the sliced onions. Arrange half of the clams on top. Season with salt and pepper. Repeat with remaining potatoes, onion and clams. Season again. Sprinkle with bacon scraps and rendered fat. Pour over all, the 2 cups of liquid. Bake in 325F oven for 1 hour. Prepare sufficient pastry crust for a 2-crust pie. (See our *"Flaky Pastry"* recipe on page 67). Remove pan from oven and cover with pastry. Prick pastry to allow steam to escape. Return to a 450F oven for 20 minutes, or until pastry is lightly browned. Makes 8 servings.

Maritime Quiche

2 medium tomatoes
1 cup French salad dressing
1 pound smoked fish fillets
1 cup milk
3 cups cooked rice
2 tablespoons butter, melted
1 cup grated Canadian Cheddar cheese
1/4 cup chopped chives
3 eggs, beaten

Preheat oven to 350F. Cut the tomatoes in six wedges each and cover with French dressing. Set tomatoes aside and allow to marinate. Meanwhile, cut the fish fillets into pieces 2 to 3 inches long. Place in a shallow baking dish. Add milk. Bake in 350F oven for 20 minutes, or until fish flakes with a fork. Drain, reserving 3/4 cup liquid. Grease a 9-inch pie plate. Make rice crust combining the cooked rice, butter and one egg. Turn into pie plate and press firmly and evenly over bottom, sides and rim to form a pie shell. Sprinkle ½ cup of cheddar cheese over shell. Arrange cooked fish on top and sprinkle with an additional ½ cup of grated cheese. Combine reserved poaching liquid with the two remaining eggs. Pour into pie plate. Bake in 350F oven for 30 minutes. Remove from oven and arrange drained tomato wedges around edge of filling, skin side up. Return pie to oven and bake for 10 minutes longer, or until custard is set. Garnish with finely chopped chives or green onion tops. Serve piping hot. Makes 6 servings.

Fisherman's Trout

Prepare a bed of glowing coals. Clean Trout. Wrap in fern leaves. Pack each in mud, ½ to 1 inch thick. Make a pit in the centre of the coals. Lay mud-wrapped fish in pit and cover with coals.
Requires 45 minutes to 1 hour to cook, when the dried mud begins to crack off. If desired, sprinkle with salt, pepper and lemon juice.

Creamed Oysters

1 pint oysters
2 ½ tbsp flour
½ tsp salt
Cayenne
3 tbsp butter
1 cup rich milk
⅓ cup oyster juice
⅛ tsp celery salt

Clean oysters; cook until plump in oyster juice; drain.
Make white sauce; add oysters.
Serve on toast or in timbale cases.

Grapefruit Crab Cocktail

1 can grapefruit sections
1 can 6 ½ ounce crab meat
1 cup mayonnaise
2 tbsp. vinegar
1 tsp. lemon juice, fresh, frozen, or canned
1 drop Tabasco sauce

Chill grapefruit and crab meat in cans. Drain grapefruit. Flake crab meat, removing bony tissue. Alternate grapefruit and crab meat in cocktail glasses. Mix in remaining ingredients; pour over grapefruit and crab meat. Makes 8 servings.

Megan Follows and Schuyler Grant in "Anne of Green Gables - The Continuing Story"

Main Course

Can you imagine anything as lovely as an autumn picnic on the stately grounds of an estate, complete with silver dishes and tea service? In such a setting, it is difficult to prepare a main course as the pinnacle of a meal since the delicious roast or succulent chicken will not likely be remembered as much as the experience of dining out of doors. No culinary wizardry deserves to be upstaged by breathtaking scenery. Or if you are anything like Anne, a wild sheep chase! Take heed to contain your main course to the confines of an elegant table setting.

Braised Short Ribs with Vegetables

2 pounds short ribs
3 tablespoons flour
2 tablespoons margarine or oil
2 teaspoons salt
1/8 teaspoon pepper
2 small onions, sliced
2 carrots, sliced
2 potatoes, quartered
1/2 cup celery, diced
1/2 cup water

Mix the salt and pepper into the flour. Cut the short ribs into squares and dredge in the seasoned flour. Once the oil is very hot in the pan, add the ribs and brown on all sides. Add the water to the pan and simmer 2 hours, this will make the ribs tender. Add the vegetables and cook 30 minutes or until vegetables are soft and the sauce is thickened.

Beef Birds

2 pounds steak, cut thin
2 cups bread dressing
1/4 cup flour
1 teaspoon salt
1/4 teaspoon pepper
2 tablespoons margarine or oil
1 cup sour cream

Cut the steak into 3 x 4 inch pieces. Dredge the pieces in the flour seasoned with the salt and pepper. Place the bread dressing in the middle of each piece. Roll the steak to enclose the dressing and skewer or tie in place. Brown the steak rolls in the hot oil. Once browned, turn the heat down to low, add the sour cream and cover tightly. Simmer or bake for 2 hours. Thicken the liquid, if need be, using flour and water. Remove the skewers or string and serve.

Corned Beef & Cabbage

1 (3 to 4 pound) corned beef brisket
1 medium-sized onion, sliced
1 bay leaf
2 garlic cloves
1 teaspoon celery seeds
6 peppercorns
1 head cabbage

In a large saucepan combine corned beef brisket, onion, bay leaf, garlic cloves, celery seeds and peppercorns. Bring to a boil and simmer for 3 hours, or until tender. Cut cabbage head in wedges. Add to meat, and simmer 12 to 14 minutes longer. Makes 6 to 8 servings.

Veal Chops with Mushrooms

6 veal loin or rib chops
1/3 cup butter or margarine
3/4 cup fresh mushrooms
2 tablespoons lemon juice
1/2 cup sliced onion
1/2 clove, crushed garlic
1/4 cup flour
1 teaspoon salt
1/4 teaspoon pepper
1 1/4 cups condensed beef broth
2/3 cup dry white wine
1 teaspoon chopped tarragon
1 teaspoon liquid gravy seasoning
1/2 teaspoon snipped chives

Wipe chops with damp paper towels. With hot butter in a deep skillet, brown chops on both sides. Remove chops; put in casserole. Sprinkle mushrooms with lemon juice. Add mushrooms with onions and garlic to drippings in the pan. Saute until golden - about 5 minutes. Remove with slotted spoon and set aside with chops. Stir flour, salt & pepper into pan drippings until well blended. Gradually stir in bouillon and wine. Add tarragon, gravy seasoning, chives and pepper. Bring to boiling, stirring; pour over chops & vegetables in casserole. Cover & bake 30 to 40 minutes at 350F.

German Schnitzel

2 pounds veal cutlet
1 egg, slightly beaten
1 tablespoon milk
½ cup flour
¼ teaspoon salt
a pinch of pepper
1 ½ cups bread crumbs
butter

Cut veal into serving portions and pound to slightly flatten. Chill the cutlets thoroughly. In a shallow dish, combine egg and milk. In another shallow dish combine flour, crumbs, salt and pepper. Dip the chilled veal in the egg mixture followed by the crumb mixture. Let the cutlets dry for 30 minutes. Heat the butter on high and then add cutlets and fry until golden brown. This is traditionally served with sliced lemon and a fried egg on top. Makes 6 to 8 servings.

Stuffed Lamb Shanks

6 lamb shanks
2 tablespoons oil
2 cups vegetable stock or water
1 teaspoon salt
⅛ teaspoon pepper
½ cup rice
½ cup celery, chopped

Brown the lamb shanks in the hot oil. Add stock and seasonings, cover tightly and simmer until tender (about 1 hour). Remove the shanks. While the meat is cooling, cook the rice using the lamb stock. Once the shanks are cooled, pull the bone out carefully so as not to break the meat. Combine the cooked rice and celery, and stuff into the shanks (where the bones previously were). Place the stuffed shanks in a casserole and cover with thickened stock. Heat before serving at 350F for 30 minutes.

Curried Lamb

3 slices side bacon, diced
½ cup celery, sliced
1 medium onion, finely chopped
2 tablespoons flour
1 tablespoon curry powder
¾ teaspoon salt
½ teaspoon turmeric
½ cup water
1 cup milk
2 cubes chicken bouillon
½ cup sweetened applesauce
2 teaspoons sugar
2 teaspoons lemon juice
2 cups cooked lamb, cubed

Cook the bacon until crisp and then add the celery and onion and cook on medium for 5 more minutes. Remove from heat and stir in flour, curry, salt and turmeric. Next add water, milk and bouillon cubes, stirring well to incorporate. Return to heat and stir constantly, until thickened. Stir in applesauce, sugar, lemon juice and lamb. Cover and simmer for 10 minutes. Serve over hot fluffy rice and garnish with shredded coconut. Serves 4.

Apple Pork Chops

6 pork chops, ¾ inch thick
salt and pepper, to taste
6 tablespoons maple sugar
2 tablespoons flour
1 cup apple juice
3 apples

Sear the pork chops in oil on high heat. Season with salt and pepper. Mix maple sugar and flour and sprinkle over chops. Add the apple juice and simmer covered over medium heat for 20 minutes. Core the apples and cut in half, but do not peel. Place one half apple on each chop. Cover and cook for an additional 20 minutes or until apples are soft and sauce is thick and smooth. Makes 6 servings.

Ham in Milk

2 large pieces (1 inch thick) sliced cooked ham
1 teaspoon dry mustard
3 tablespoons brown sugar
2 cups milk
6 whole cloves
2 bay leaves

Preheat oven to 300F. Trim off excess fat from ham and place in shallow casserole. Combine the mustard and brown sugar and spread over ham. Add milk, cloves and bay leaves. Cover, and bake in 300F oven for 30 minutes. Uncover, and bake for 30 minutes longer. Remove from liquid and cut in serving portions. Makes 4 - 6 servings.

Chicken with Ginger & Honey

1 (2 $\frac{1}{2}$ to 3 lb.) chicken
2 tablespoons butter
$\frac{1}{2}$ cup honey
$\frac{1}{2}$ cup water
$\frac{1}{4}$ cup butter, melted
$\frac{1}{4}$ cup lemon juice
1 teaspoon ground ginger

Cut the chicken into serving pieces. In a heavy frying pan melt the 2 tablespoons of butter and add the chicken, quickly browning on all sides. Combine the remaining ingredients and pour over the browned chicken. Cover and cook over low heat, basting occasionally for 35 to 40 minutes, or until chicken is tender. Makes 5 to 6 servings.

Coq au Vin

1 (4 lb.) chicken
salt & white pepper, to taste
$\frac{1}{2}$ cup bacon, diced
2 tablespoons butter
12 small onions
$\frac{1}{2}$ pound button mushrooms
$\frac{1}{4}$ cup green onion, finely chopped
1 clove garlic, crushed
3 tablespoons flour

½ cup water
2 cups red wine

In seasoning pouch:
2 stalks celery
2 sprigs parsley
½ bay leaf
3 peppercorns
1 whole clove
¼ teaspoon thyme

Cut the chicken into serving pieces and season with salt and pepper. Fry bacon until crisp and then remove from heat and drain pieces on paper towels. Pour out all but 3 tablespoons of the bacon fat from the frying pan. Return the pan to heat along with the onions and mushrooms. Cover and cook for 5 minutes or until onions begin to brown slightly. Remove cover. Add green onion and garlic. Cook for 1 minute being careful not to burn the garlic. Stir in the flour and cook until browned. Gradually add the water and wine. Continue cooking, stirring constantly, until smooth. Return the chicken to pan. In a cheesecloth bag combine all the seasoning ingredients. Tie bag closed and then add to pan. Add the cooked bacon to pan. Cover and bring to a boil. Reduce heat and simmer for 45 to 60 minutes or until chicken is tender. To serve, arrange chicken and vegetables on a platter. Skim any excess fat from sauce and remove cheesecloth bag. If sauce is too thin, boil over high heat and reduce to desired consistency. Pour sauce over chicken and garnish with fresh parsley. Makes 4 servings.

Tourtière

½ pound ground pork
½ pound ground beef
1 onion, chopped
2-3 medium potatoes
¼ cup water, if necessary
1 teaspoon salt
¼ teaspoon pepper
1 teaspoon sage

Cook the pork, beef and onion over medium heat until meat has lost its pink color, adding water if necessary. Cook and mash potatoes. Add potatoes and seasonings to meat mixture. Line two 8 inch pie pans with pastry (See *"Flaky Pastry"* recipe on page 67) and fill with meat mixture. Cover with top crust and bake in 425F oven for 20 to 25 minutes.

Cabbage Rolls

1 pound minced lean beef
1 teaspoon salt
½ teaspoon pepper
1 egg, beaten
¼ cup diced onions
¼ cup diced green pepper
2 tablespoons chili sauce
¼ cup melted butter
½ cup rice
2 tablespoons sugar
1 tablespoon lemon juice
1 large cabbage

Sauce:
1 can stewed tomatoes
1 teaspoon sugar
1 can tomato soup
salt and pepper to taste

Finely mince the onions, pepper and tomatoes and mix well with remaining ingredients except for the cabbage. Simmer cabbage leaves to soften them. Roll mixture in warm leaves. Arrange in 2 inch deep pan. Pour the sauce over the rolls and bake in 325F oven for 3 to 4 hours.

Kate Lynch, Megan Follows, Genevieve Appleton and Wendy Hiller in "Anne of Green Gables - The Sequel"

Vegetables

Although some of us may prefer to skip our vegetables altogether and go straight to dessert, you probably wouldn't break a chalkboard over a person's head if they called you broccoli - or carrots. Unfortunately for Mr. Gilbert Blythe, he found the one individual who was sensitive to "vegetable" references. Of course the real reason Anne abhorred the name *"Carrots"* was because she felt it mocked her hair colour. She so despised the brilliant shade of red that she dyed it green. Good thing Gil didn't move on to call her *"Brussel Sprouts"*...

Scalloped Sweet Potatoes

5 sweet potatoes
½ cup brown sugar
1 teaspoon salt
½ teaspoon ground cinnamon
2 tablespoons butter
½ cup boiling water
6 to 8 marshmallows

Preheat oven to 350F. Boil sweet potatoes in a little water until tender. Peel and cut into ½ inch slices. Arrange slices in a buttered baking dish, sprinkling each layer with brown sugar, salt and cinnamon, which have been mixed together. Dot with butter. Pour boiling water over the potatoes. Bake in a 350F oven for 20 minutes or until top is golden brown. Remove and arrange marshmallows over top. Bake again about 5 minutes, until marshmallows are puffed and brown. Serves 6.

Scalloped Potatoes with Leeks

3 medium potatoes, thinly sliced
3 leeks, white part only, finely chopped
pinch salt and pepper
1 ½ cups light cream
¾ cup grated Gruyere cheese

Pre-heat oven to 350F. In a buttered 2-quart (2 litre) casserole dish, layer with potatoes and leeks. Sprinkle with salt and pepper on top. Repeat until you have three layers of each. Pour in the cream and spread the cheese over the top. Bake for 1 hour until potatoes are tender and the cheese is slightly browned.

German Style Dumplings

4 medium potatoes
1 cooked and mashed potato
¼ cup all-purpose flour
1 ¼ teaspoon salt
1 egg, well beaten
2 tablespoons butter
2 medium Spanish onions, chopped
1 cup milk

Peel and finely grate 4 potatoes. Press with paper towel to extract excess water. Combine with a mashed potato, flour, beaten egg and 1 teaspoon of salt. Form this mixture into dumplings about 2 inches in diameter. Boil for 20 to 25 minutes in salted water. Makes about 8 dumplings. For sauce: melt butter in a saucepan and add onions. Saute until transparent, then stir in milk and ¼ teaspoon of salt. Simmer until onion is soft, then pour over cooked dumplings.

Potato Cakes

1 ½ pounds potatoes, cooked & peeled
1 clove garlic, peeled
½ pound Farmer cheese, crumbled
1 teaspoon salt
a pinch of freshly-ground pepper
2 small eggs
2 cups flour or some finely-ground toasted bread crumbs
1 to 2 cups peanut or safflower oil (½" deep in frying pan)

Shred the potatoes using the fine disk of a food mill. Crush the garlic in a garlic press and add it to the potatoes with the cheese, salt and pepper. Beat the eggs together well and work them into the potato mixture. Form the mixture into 12 small cakes, each about 2 to 3 inches across and half an inch thick. Pat a little flour or bread crumbs on the outside of the cakes. Heat the oil until very hot, but not so hot that it smokes. Fry the potato cakes for 3 to 5 minutes on each side. Drain them on brown paper towel and serve immediately with a spicy tomato salsa. After the cakes have been fried, you can keep them hot in a 400F oven for about 15 to 20 minutes. After which, they may dry out. To test the heat of the fat, put a wooden spoon into it. If the fat sizzles around it, then it is hot enough to put in the potato cakes. If the fat is too hot, the outside of the potato cakes will start to crumble and they will color too quickly on the outside, without heating right through.

Seasoned Carrots

2 tablespoons butter
5 medium carrots, coarsely grated (3 cups)
2 green onions, finely chopped
2 sprigs of parsley, finely chopped
1 sprig of rosemary, finely chopped
salt and pepper, to taste

Melt the butter in a large frying pan. Add the carrots and cook on high heat for 3 minutes, stirring constantly. Stir in remaining ingredients and cook 1 minute. Season and serve hot.
Serves 2 to 3.

Buttery Tomatoes

1/4 cup butter, softened
1 teaspoon icing sugar
1 tablespoon finely minced onion
1/4 teaspoon salt
1/2 teaspoon dry mustard
a pinch of cayenne
4 tomatoes

Pre-heat the oven to 350F. Cream the butter into a small bowl and add all other ingredients except tomatoes. Cut the tomatoes in half and dot them with the buttery mixture. Bake in oven for 20 minutes.

Fiddleheads

2 tablespoons butter
3 cups fiddleheads
1 teaspoon lemon juice
1/2 teaspoon salt
a pinch of pepper

Remove the brown sheath and scales of the fiddleheads. Wash thoroughly in warm water. Cook in boiling water for 10 to 15 minutes or until tender.
Drain and add other ingredients. Serves 4.

Turnip Apple Casserole

1 medium turnip
1/4 cup butter
a pinch of salt and pepper
2 cups sliced and peeled apples (Northern Spies are best)
1/2 cup brown sugar
2 tablespoons all-purpose flour

Pre-heat the oven to 350F. Cut turnip into pieces and boil until tender. Remove from the heat and add half of the butter, salt and pepper. Whip with an electric beater until light and soft. Let cool. Toss apples with brown sugar. Butter a 2-quart (2L) casserole dish. Put a layer of turnip in the bottom, then a layer of apple. Repeat, ending with a layer of turnip on top. Combine the flour, remaining butter and brown sugar together and sprinkle on top. Bake uncovered for 1 hour. Serves 6.

Glazed Squash Rings

2 acorn squash
½ cup corn syrup
¼ cup orange juice
1 tablespoon grated orange rind
2 tablespoons butter

Preheat oven to 375F. Wash squash and cut into ½ inch rings. Arrange in a single layer in a baking pan. Add water and cover with foil to steam in the oven for 10 minutes. Combine the other ingredients in a saucepan and boil. Remove from heat. Drain the squash rings and sprinkle with salt and pepper. Pour glaze over the rings and return to the oven. Bake for 30 minutes longer, basting frequently. Makes 6 servings.

Old-Style Succotash

12 large ears of corn
1 cup shelled green beans
5 cups boiling water
1 cup cream (10% m.g)
3 tablespoons butter
1 teaspoon salt
¼ teaspoon pepper

Husk and silk the corn. Slice the kernels thinly from the cobs, scraping thoroughly. Place the cobs in a large saucepan with green beans and boiling water. Cook for 30 minutes or until beans are very tender. Remove cobs and scrape a second time. Add corn kernels and cook for 10 minutes. Stir in other ingredients and season to taste. Serves 10.

Quick Succotash

1 ½ cups cooked, drained green lima beans
1 ½ cups cooked, drained whole kernel corn
2 tablespoons butter
½ cup cream (10% m.g.)
1 teaspoon salt
a pinch of pepper

Combine all ingredients and heat until butter has melted. Season to taste. Serves 6.

Zucchini Quiche

3 cups thinly sliced zucchini
1 small onion, chopped
1 cup biscuit mix
4 large eggs
½ cup vegetable oil
½ cup grated Parmesan cheese
½ cup grated Gruyere cheese
½ teaspoon dried marjoram
2 sprigs chopped parsley
¼ teaspoon salt
a pinch of pepper

Preheat the oven to 350F. Mix all the ingredients in a large bowl. Place in a greased 3 litre casserole dish. Bake for 30 minutes or until golden. Serves 8.

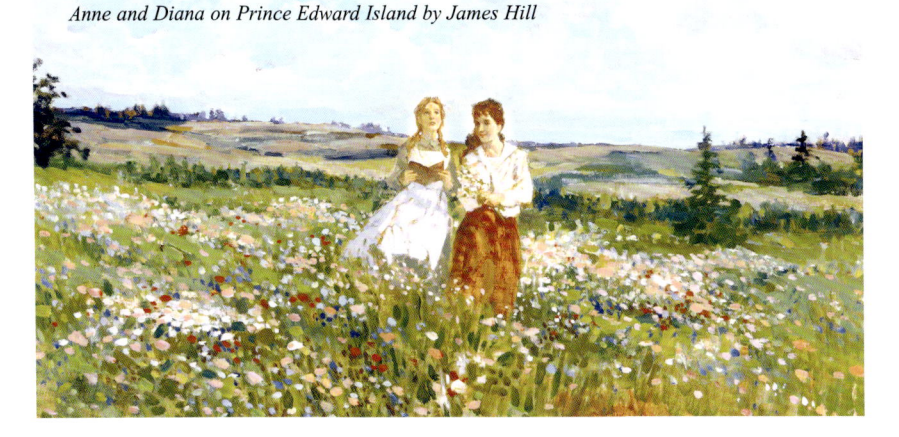

Anne and Diana on Prince Edward Island by James Hill

Salads

Even salads were not a tame course in Avonlea where one needed to fend off ravenous cows if one hoped to harvest enough cabbage from the garden for decent coleslaw. Although the welfare of cabbages was a larger priority for Rachel Lynde, Anne got herself into a real mess when she vowed to keep her delinquent Jersey, *Dolly*, away from Rachel's prized patch. Anne and Diana ended up with plenty of dirt and egg on their faces when they chased the offending cow through a muddy field; then in frustration sold the animal on the spot to the farmers' market. Unfortunately, the cow turned out to be Rachel's and Dolly was still safe in her pen where Anne had left her. More salad?

Cucumber Yogurt Salad

¼ cup olive oil
juice of ½ lemon or 1 lime
a pinch of salt
a pinch of pepper
3 large green onions, chopped
2 tablespoons fresh chopped dill
1 medium cucumber
1 cup unflavored yogurt
½ cup whole black olives

In a salad bowl, combine citrus juice, olive oil, green onions, dill, salt and pepper. Peel and slice the cucumber, adding it to the dressing until pieces are coated. Add the yogurt and mix again. Let stand in the refrigerator for 1 hour to allow flavors to blend. Garnish with black olives and serve. Serves 4.

Leeks Vinaigrette

3 leeks, (white part only), cleaned and thinly sliced
2 teaspoons capers, chopped
2 tablespoons lemon juice
¼ cup olive oil
½ teaspoon granulated sugar
1 teaspoon Dijon mustard
1 clove garlic, minced
a pinch of salt
a pinch of pepper
1 tablespoon fresh parsley, chopped
1 tablespoon chopped cress

Toss together the leeks and capers in a small bowl. Mix all other ingredients in a jar, cover and shake vigorously. Pour dressing over the leeks/capers and chill in the refrigerator for 2 hours. Serves 4.

Dandelion Salad

4 cups lightly packed dandelion leaves
3 slices bacon
1 small onion, finely chopped
1 teaspoon brown sugar
1 tablespoon white vinegar
2 tablespoons sour cream
¼ teaspoon pepper

Wash and carefully drain dandelion leaves, then place them in a bowl. Cook the bacon in a frying pan until crisp. Remove bacon and drain on a paper towel. Briefly cook the onion in the bacon fat. Add brown sugar and stir until dissolved. Remove from heat and add vinegar. Let cool for 10 minutes and add sour cream while stirring slowly. Let stand until room temperature. Sprinkle dressing over the leaves and crumble the bacon on top. Lightly dust the top with pepper and serve. Serves 4.

Green Salad

1 small head lettuce
½ cup chopped celery
⅓ chopped green pepper
1 ¼ cups water chestnuts, sliced
¼ cup chopped red onion
1 ¼ cups frozen peas
2 cups mayonnaise
1 teaspoon granulated sugar
½ cup grated Romano cheese

In the order specified, lay the vegetables in a bowl. Cover with mayonnaise and sprinkle with sugar. Grate the cheese over the salad. Cover and store in refrigerator. No need to toss the salad, just serve as is! Serves 8-10.

Carrot Salad

2 lb. carrots, sliced diagonally (6 cups)
1 green pepper, thinly sliced
1 large onion, thinly sliced

Dressing:
½ cup vegetable oil
1 can (10oz.) tomato soup
¾ cup white vinegar
1 teaspoon Worcestershire sauce
1 teaspoon dry mustard
1 cup white sugar
1 teaspoon fresh basil or tarragon, finely chopped

In a large bowl, combine carrots, pepper and onions. In another bowl mix the dressing ingredients. Pour dressing over vegetables and refrigerate, covered, for at least 24 hours. This should keep up to two weeks in the refrigerator. Serve chilled or at room temperature. Serves 6 to 8.

Cabbage Salad

½ cup vegetable oil
¾ cup white vinegar
¾ cup granulated sugar
1 teaspoon salt
1 teaspoon celery seed
1 teaspoon mustard seed
1 medium cabbage, shredded
1 onion, chopped
2 green peppers, chopped
2 carrots, shredded
½ cup pitted and chopped green olives

In a saucepan combine the oil, vinegar, sugar and spices. Bring to a boil and allow to cool until lukewarm. In a bowl, mix the fresh vegetables. Pour the liquid over the vegetables and let sit for 10 minutes before serving. Lift from the liquid and drain slightly when serving. Accompany with a creamy dressing, as desired.

Bean Salad

1 cup granulated sugar
½ cup water
1 ½ cups white vinegar
1 ¾ cups canned and sliced green beans
1 ¾ cups canned and sliced yellow wax beans
1 ¼ cups canned lima beans
1 cup chickpeas
3 stalks celery, thinly sliced
3 onions, thinly sliced
1 green pepper, thinly sliced
1 sweet red pepper, thinly sliced

Bring the sugar, water and vinegar to a boil in a small saucepan. Drain the canned beans and rinse. Combine beans and vegetables in a bowl and pour sauce over them. Refrigerate 24 hours before serving. Serves 10.

Mom's Potato Salad

10 medium potatoes
1 tablespoon and 1 pinch salt
½ cup granulated sugar
1 ½ teaspoons all-purpose flour
1 teaspoon dry mustard
1 egg
⅓ cup cider vinegar
3 tablespoons water
a pinch of pepper
2 tablespoons butter
1 onion, finely chopped
8 radishes, thinly sliced
2 stalks celery, finely chopped
¼ green pepper, finely chopped
3 hard boiled eggs
3 sprigs fresh parsley

Boil the potatoes and peel them while warm. Chop into cubes and sprinkle with salt before placing them in the refrigerator to cool. Combine the sugar, flour and mustard in the top part of a double boiler. In a small bowl beat an egg slightly and add the vinegar and water. Add the liquid to the dry ingredients very slowly and stir gently until blended. Add salt and pepper to taste. Heat the mixture until it thickens then remove from heat before adding the butter. Refrigerate right away. When the potatoes have cooled, add the onion, radishes, celery, green pepper and two of the hard-boiled eggs that have been thinly sliced. Gently mix all together while slowly adding the dressing. Allow to sit in the refrigerator for further cooling and setting. The longer you let it sit, the better it gets! Garnish before serving with the sprigs of parsley and the third boiled egg, thinly sliced . Serves 10-12.

Moulded Beef Salad Ring

2 envelopes unflavoured gelatine
½ cup cold water
3 ½ cups canned diced beets
1½ cups beet liquid
½ cup granulated sugar
1½ teaspoon salt
½ cup white vinegar
1¼ cups finely diced celery

1 tablespoon finely chopped onion
2 tablespoons prepared horseradish

Soften gelatin in water. Drain and reserve liquid from the diced beets. Finally chop the beets into 3 ½ cups. Set aside until needed. Measure ½ cup of beet liquid into a saucepan and blend in the granulated sugar, salt and white vinegar. Bring to a boil, add the softened gelatine and stir until dissolved. Remove from heat. Chill until slightly thickened. Fold in chopped beets with celery, chopped onion and horseradish. Pour into an oiled 6-cup ring mould or 8 individual moulds. Chill until set, preferably overnight for the large mould. To serve, unmold on salad greens and fill center with cottage cheese. Serve with cucumber mayonnaise. Makes 8 to 10 servings.

Lobster Salad

3 freshly boiled and shelled lobsters
3 hard cooked eggs, chopped
½ cup sweet pickles, chopped
½ cup mayonnaise
½ small onion, finely minced
½ teaspoon salt
½ pinch pepper

Cut the lobster into bite size pieces. Gently mix all of the ingredients together. Place on a leaf of lettuce and serve. Serves 4

Fisherman's Delight

2 cups water
2 tablespoons lemon juice
½ teaspoon salt
1 bay leaf
1 teaspoon instant minced onion
1 pound fresh or frozen (thawed) scallops
4 to 5 medium potatoes
1 cup fresh or frozen cut green beans
1 cup mayonnaise
½ cup sour cream
¼ cup chopped green onions
¼ cup chopped parsley
½ teaspoon dried dillweed
1 tablespoon horseradish
1 cup thinly sliced celery

In a saucepan combine water, lemon juice, salt, bay leaf, and instant minced onion. Bring to a boil and add the scallops. Reduce heat, cover and simmer for 5 minutes. Drain and cut scallops in halves and quarters, depending on size. Cook the potatoes until tender. Cool, and slice ¼ inch thick. Cook green beans until tender. Marinate for at least 2 hours the scallops, potatoes and beans separately in a small amount of oil and vinegar dressing (avoid using a red or tomato-base dressing). Keep in refrigerator. Combine scallops, potatoes and beans with a mixture of mayonnaise, sour cream, green onions, chopped parsley, dried dillweed, horseradish and celery.

Toss gently and arrange in lettuce-lined serving bowl. Garnish with cherry tomatoes or tomato wedges and lemon slices.

Makes 8 servings.

Mandarin Orange Salad

½ cup sugar
¼ cup vinegar
1 cup vegetable oil
1 tsp. salt
½ small red onion, chopped
1 tsp. dry mustard
2 tbsp. water
1 head romaine lettuce
10 oz can mandarin orange segments
½ cup silvered almonds, toasted

Sweet Mustard Dressing: Blend sugar, vinegar, oil, salt, onion, dry mustard and water in a blender until well mixed. Refrigerate for a few hours to enable the ingredients to blend the flavours.

Tear lettuce into bite size pieces and place in salad bowl. Just before serving, add the oranges and almonds and toss with enough dressing to coat the leaves. You will probably have some dressing left over. It keeps well in a covered glass jar in the refrigerator.

Variation: Use fresh strawberries.

Sweet Pickled Beets

2 cups sugar
2 cups water
2 cups vinegar
1 tsp. whole allspice
1 tsp. whole cloves

Boil all ingredients for 15 minutes. Cook, clean and slice beets. Put in jars. Pour vinegar mixture over beets. Cool and keep in fridge.

Anne Shirley on Prince Edward Island by James Hill

Desserts

Truly the most delightful part of a complete meal, the dessert can be the crowning achievement, when you approach it with care. For Anne this would have meant not pretending to be a nun with a cheese cloth that was intended to protect plum pudding sauce from inquisitive mice. Poor Anne was probably more upset than the mouse that inevitably drowned in the decadent sauce because as she commented, "...in the end it was a romantic way to perish, for a mouse."

Flaky Pastry

2 cups pastry (soft wheat) flour or 1¾ cups all-purpose flour
¾ teaspoon salt
⅔ cup shortening or lard
4 to 5 tablespoons cold water

Blend together flour and salt. Using a pastry blender or two knives cut ⅓ cup shortening or lard in until very fine. Then cut in the remaining ⅓ cup shortening or lard until the size of peas. Stir in the cold water a tablespoon at a time. Use just enough water to make a dough that will cling together and clean easily from the bowl. Divide in half. Roll each portion out on a lightly floured surface, rolling from the center of the dough to the outside edge. (This will keep it round in shape). Extra pastry may be wrapped in plastic wrap or wax paper and stored in refrigerator. Makes sufficient pastry for one 9 inch by 2 inch pie crust, two 9 inch pie shells, or 12 to 14 medium-sized tart shells.

Old-Fashioned Molasses Tarts

1½ cups all-purpose flour
½ teaspoon allspice
½ teaspoon cinnamon
a pinch of cloves
a pinch of salt
½ cup shortening
¼ cup molasses
2 to 3 tablespoons cold water
12 cups blueberry jam

Preheat oven to 425F. Sift or blend together flour, allspice, cinnamon, cloves and salt. With a pastry blender or two knives, cut in the shortening and with a fork stir in the molasses and 2 to 3 tablespoons of cold water. Roll dough out on a lightly floured surface. Cut with a floured cookie cutter and line about 2 dozen small-sized muffin cups. Fill tart shells ⅔ full with blueberry jam. Bake in 425F oven for 12 to 15 minutes, or until brown. Makes 2 dozen tarts.

Homespun Pie

3 cups grated raw potato
2 cups grated raw apple
2 cups raisins
2 cups lightly packed brown sugar
½ cup mixed peel
½ cup molasses
½ cup vinegar
3 cups hot water
1½ teaspoons salt
2 teaspoons nutmeg
2 teaspoons cinnamon
3 tablespoons butter

Preheat oven to 450F. Prepare sufficient pastry for a 2-crust 9 inch pie. Roll out half the dough, line pie plate and trim. Roll out top crust. Combine in a four-quart saucepan the potato, apple, raisins, brown sugar, mixed peel, molasses, vinegar, hot water, salt, nutmeg, cinnamon, and butter. Simmer slowly over low heat for about 30 minutes, or until thick. Watch carefully as the mixture burns easily. Makes sufficient for 4 pies. Remainder may be sealed hot in sterilized jars for future use. Turn 4 cups filling into pastry-lined pie plate. Cover with top crust. Seal and flute edges and slit or prick top crust. Bake in 450F over for 10 minutes, or until pastry is golden. Reduce heat to 350F and bake for 30 minutes longer.

Maple Syrup Pie

2 eggs
1 cup lightly packed brown sugar
2 tablespoons flour
1 cup maple syrup
2 tablespoons butter, melted
½ cup coarsely chopped nuts
1 teaspoon vanilla
pinch salt

Preheat oven to 450F. Prepare sufficient pastry and line a 9-inch pie plate. Trim and flute the edge, but do not prick. Slightly beat the 2 eggs, then mix together and blend in the brown sugar and flour. Stir in the maple syrup, butter, chopped nuts, vanilla and salt. Pour into prepared pie shell. Bake in 400F oven for 35 to 40 minutes, or until filling is set. Cool before serving.

Apple Cream Pie

⅔ cup sugar
2 tablespoons flour
⅛ teaspoon salt
1 cup sour cream
1 egg, slightly beaten
1 teaspoon pure vanilla extract
2 cups finely chopped apples
one 9-inch unbaked pie shell

Topping:
⅓ cup flour
⅓ cup sugar
1 teaspoon cinnamon
¼ cup butter or margarine

Combine sugar, flour and salt. Add cream, egg, vanilla and beat until smooth. Add chopped apples and pour into unbaked pie shell. For topping combine flour, sugar and cinnamon and cut in butter or margarine. Sprinkle over top of pie. Bake in a 425F oven for 25-30 minutes. Serves 6.

Sour Cream Coffee Cake

1 ⅓ cups pastry (soft wheat) flour
2 teaspoons baking powder
1 teaspoon baking soda
½ cup butter
1 cup granulated sugar
2 eggs
1 teaspoon vanilla
1 cup thick dairy sour cream
¼ cup lightly packed brown sugar
1 tablespoon cinnamon
2 tablespoons finely chopped nuts

Preheat oven to 350F. Grease thoroughly an 8-inch square cake pan. Dust lightly with flour. Sift together pastry flour, baking powder and baking soda. Then blend together butter and sugar. Beat in eggs and vanilla. Beat until light and fluffy. Add sifted dry ingredients to creamed mixture alternately with sour cream. Combine lightly after each addition. Spread half the batter a prepared pan. Sprinkle with half of a mixture of brown sugar, cinnamon and chopped nuts. Cover with remaining batter. Sprinkle with remainder of topping. Bake in 350F oven for 45 to 50 minutes. Serve warm. May be wrapped in foil and reheated. Makes one cake.

Oatmeal Cake

1¼ cup boiling water
1 cup quick-cooking oats
½ cup margarine
1 cup white sugar
1 cup brown sugar, firmly packed
2 eggs, unbeaten
1 teaspoon cinnamon
1 teaspoon vanilla
1½ cup flour
1 teaspoon baking soda

Pour boiling water over oats and let stand 20 minutes. Cream margarine with white and brown sugar, beat in eggs, and add cinnamon and vanilla. Blend in flour and soda, then add oats and mix well. Pour into 8 by 16 inch pan. Bake 45 minutes at 350F.

Frosting:
3 teaspoons butter
⅔ cup brown sugar
1 cup coconut, shredded
1 cup chopped nuts
2 eggs

Mix all ingredients, blending well. Pour over hot cake, then return to oven for 5 to 10 minutes or until brown. Goes well with cream or ice cream.

Rhubarb Cake

2 cups flour
1 teaspoon baking soda
¼ teaspoon salt
1½ cups light brown sugar
½ cup margarine
1 egg
1 cup milk
1 teaspoon vanilla extract

2½ cups rhubarb, cut in 1" pieces
½ cup granulated sugar
1 teaspoon cinnamon

Mix flour, soda and salt then it set aside. In large mixing bowl, cream brown sugar and margarine until fluffy. Beat in egg. At low speed, beat in flour mixture alternately with milk until well blended. Stir in vanilla and rhubarb. Turn into greased and floured 13 by 9 by 2 inch pan. Sprinkle with a mixture of cinnamon and sugar. Bake at 350F for 40 minutes.

Walnut Chocolate Cake

½ pound butter
6 whole eggs
1 cup flour
2 cups yellow sugar
1 cup walnut pieces
1 teaspoon cocoa
1 teaspoon baking powder

Sift together flour, baking powder and cocoa. Cream together butter, sugar and eggs until light and fluffy. Add flour mixture slowly. Fold in nuts. Line oblong pan with waxed paper. Bake at 350F for 45 minutes or until cake tester inserted in centre comes out clean. Cool before using your favourite icing.

Queen's Cake

1 cup boiling water
1 cup dates, chopped
1 teaspoon baking soda
¼ cup butter
1 cup granulated sugar
1 egg
1 teaspoon vanilla
1½ cups flour
1 teaspoon baking powder
¼ to ½ teaspoon salt

Let boiling water, dates and baking soda stand until cool, then add butter, granulated sugar, egg and vanilla which has been beaten until fluffy. Mix into date mixture into 3 sections with flour, baking powder and salt. For extra flavour, add one very ripe banana and ½ cup lemon juice and increase the flour by ½ cup. Bake at 350F for 1 hour.

Icing:
5 tablespoons brown sugar
3 tablespoons butter
2 tablespoons cream
½ cup coconut

Boil these ingredients 3 minutes and pour on hot cake. Return to oven and broil until topping bubbles and browns lightly.

Carrot Cake

2 cups sugar
2 cups flour
3 cups finely shredded carrots
2 teaspoons baking soda
1¼ cups vegetable oil
4 whole eggs
2 teaspoons cinnamon
a pinch of salt
2 teaspoons vanilla

Mix dry ingredients together. Blend in oil; add eggs and carrots, then vanilla. Blend well and bake in 8 inch layer pans at 350F for 35 minutes.

Icing:
1 cup cream cheese
½ cup butter
1 pound icing sugar
1 teaspoon vanilla
1 teaspoon orange juice
½ cup pecans, finely chopped

Blend cheese and butter; slowly add sugar, vanilla, orange juice and nuts. Ice only after cake is completely cold.

Apple Cake

2 large eggs
½ cup oil
¾ cup sugar
1 teaspoon vanilla
1½ cups all-purpose flour
2 teaspoons baking powder
a pinch of salt
3 tablespoons water
½ teaspoon cinnamon
3 or 4 apples, sliced and cored

Mix together eggs, oil, water and vanilla. Add sifted dry ingredients. Mix. Pour half of batter into oiled 8 inch square pan. Spread apples over batter. Sprinkle with 3 tablespoons sugar, ½ teaspoon cinnamon and 1 teaspoon flour. Spread rest of batter on top. Bake at 350F for 1 hour, or until golden brown and crusty. Other fruit mixtures can be used (blueberries, cherries, etc).

Pudding Rayon de Miel

1 cup sugar
1 cup flour
½ teaspoon baking soda
1 cup molasses
½ cup butter, melted
½ cup lukewarm milk
4 eggs, beaten

Mix sugar, flour and baking soda. Melt the butter in the milk, add the molasses to the milk and then pour all into flour mixture. Beat well before adding eggs. Pour in a well-greased tubular pan, cook in medium oven (350F) for 45 minutes. Unmold onto an attractive plate and serve warm with one of the following sauces.

Sauce d'Or

2 eggs, separated
½ to 1 cup icing sugar
⅔ teaspoon vanilla or wine
pinch salt

Beat whites of eggs until peaks are formed; add half of the sugar.

Do not wash beater. Beat yolks in a separate bowl until light in colour and thick; adding the rest of the sugar gradually. Incorporate the whites manually, without overbeating, and add flavouring.

Sauce Floradora

Use half the ingredients listed for Sauce d'Or and proceed the same way. After flavouring, add ¾ cup stiffly-beaten heavy cream (35% m.g).

Plum Pudding

½ cup regular flour, sifted
½ teaspoon baking soda
1 teaspoon ground cinnamon
½ teaspoon ground cloves
¼ teaspoon salt
¾ cup fine, dry bread crumbs
3 eggs
½ cup butter or margarine
¾ cup firmly packed light brown sugar
1 can (1 pound) purple plums, drained, pitted and chopped
1 tablespoon grated orange rind
1 cup pitted dates, cut up
1 cup seedless raisins
1 cup mixed, chopped candied fruits
1 cup chopped pecans
½ cup currants
Brandy (or Rum) Hard Sauce (see below)

Grease an 8-cup mold; dust evenly with fine sugar. Sift flour, soda, cinnamon, cloves and salt into a small bowl; stir in bread crumbs. Cream butter or margarine with brown sugar until fluffy-light in a large bowl. Beat in eggs, one at a time, then stir in plums and orange rind. Stir in flour mixture until blended; fold in dates and raisins, candied fruits, pecans and currants. Spoon into prepared mold. Cover with lid of mold, foil or waxed paper and fasten with string to hold tightly. Steam 4½ hours or until pudding is firm. Keep water boiling gently during entire cooking time, adding more boiling water if needed. If necessary, loosen around edge with a knife; invert onto a serving plate. Serve warm with the Brandy Hard Sauce.

Brandy Hard Sauce:
Beat ½ cup (1 stick) butter or margarine with 1½ cups sifted icing sugar and add brandy to taste. Cream until fluffy-light.

Oatmeal Crispies

1 cup white sugar
1 cup soft butter or margarine
1 teaspoon vanilla
1 ¼ cup sifted pastry flour
1 teaspoon salt
1 cup brown sugar
2 eggs
1 ½ cup sliced almonds (optional)
1 teaspoon soda
3 cups quick oatmeal

Cream sugars, butter, eggs and vanilla. Stir in almonds. If almonds are not used, increase oatmeal by ½ cup. Sift flour with soda and salt. Add to creamed mixture. Stir in oatmeal. Divide dough into two rolls, wrap in waxed paper and refrigerate until thoroughly chilled. Slice thin and place on lightly-greased baking sheets. Bake at 350F for 7 to 10 minutes. Makes 5 dozen cookies.

Megan Follows and Richard Farnsworth in "Anne of Green Gables"

Drinks

When Anne was busy being a good hostess by keeping Diana's glass full of raspberry cordial, she had no idea she was actually making her drunk on currant wine. As a result of her mistake, Mrs. Barry nearly ended Anne and Diana's friendship by forbidding them to associate. If you plan to serve alcoholic drinks to your guests, always serve them chilled water as well. That way they can slowly savor the drink but keep their thirst quenched - and their mothers happy!

Old Fashioned Molasses Cookies

3/4 cup sugar
1 cup shortening
1 cup molasses
1/2 teaspoon salt
1 teaspoon cloves
1 teaspoon cinnamon
2 teaspoons soda
1/2 cup boiling water
5 to 5 1/2 cups flour

Mix sugar and shortening until creamy; add molasses and mix well. Sift together flour, salt, cloves and cinnamon. Dissolve soda in boiling water and add to molasses, sugar and shortening mixture. Then add flour mixture and mix until rather stiff. Roll cookies on a floured board and cut. Bake in 350F oven until slightly browned.

Lemon Bars Deluxe

2 cups flour, sifted
1/2 cup white powdered icing sugar
1 cup butter
4 eggs, beaten
2 cups granulated sugar
1/3 cup lemon juice
1/4 cup flour
1/2 teaspoon baking powder

Sift together the flour and powdered sugar. Cut in butter until mixture clings together. Press into 13 by 9 by 2 inch pan. Bake at 350F for 20 to 25 minutes or until lightly browned. Beat together eggs, granulated sugar and lemon juice. Sift together the flour and baking powder; stir into egg mixture. Pour over baked crust. Bake at 350F for 25 minutes longer. Sprinkle with additional powdered sugar. Cool. Cut into squares.

Rhubarb Deluxe

5 pounds rhubarb
2 tablespoons grated lemon rind
14 1/2 cups water
1/3 cup lemon juice
3 cups granulated sugar

Cut the rhubarb into chunks. In a large saucepan combine rhubarb, lemon rind and water. Bring to a boil and simmer until rhubarb is tender. Stir in lemon juice. Strain through a cloth. Makes about 13 cups of juice. Stir the granulated sugar into the juice. Bring to a boil. Pour into sterilized jars and seal. Store in a cool place. Makes about 7 pints.

Lemonade

6 lemons
2 pounds granulated sugar
3 tablespoons citric acid
7 cups boiling water

Cut in half and squeeze the juice from the lemons. Cut each rind half in four. Combine lemon juice, pulp and rind with the granulated sugar and citric acid. Cover with the boiling water. Stir in until sugar is dissolved. Allow to cool. Strain and pour into sterilized jars. Store in a cool place. When serving, dilute 1 part syrup with 1 part water. Makes 6 pints syrup.

Hot Cranberry Punch

9 1/2 cups cranberry juice
Four 6-ounce cans frozen lemonade
1/2 teaspoon salt
1 teaspoon allspice
4 cups water
30 cinnamon sticks

Combine ingredients, except cinnamon sticks, in a one gallon container. Simmer gently 10 to 15 minutes. Do not boil. Serve hot in mugs, with cinnamon sticks to use as stirrers. Makes 30 one-half cup servings.

Mulled Cider

½ cup brown sugar
1 teaspoon whole allspice
1 teaspoon whole cloves
8 cups cider
¼ teaspoon salt
pinch grated nutmeg
2 orange slices
2 cinnamon sticks

Combine all of the ingredients (except the orange and cinnamon) in a saucepan and slowly bring to a boil. Cover and simmer for 20 minutes. To serve, strain into small punch cups and garnish with orange slices and cinnamon sticks.

Plum Gin

6 Damson plums
½ cup granulated sugar
3 cups gin

Prick each plum with a needle then place into a mason jar (1L). Pour in sugar then top up with gin. Do not let the gin reach as far as the metal lid. Store in a warm place for about three months, shaking periodically. When ready, strain the liquid and bottle. Serve in small amounts as you would a liqueur. The plums make remarkable treats for adults when sprinkled with icing sugar!

Raspberry Cordial

3 cups raspberries
1 cup granulated sugar
1 can frozen lemonade (thawed)
3 cups fine brandy

In a blender, puree the raspberries, sugar and lemonade. Place the puree in a large glass jar and pour the brandy over it. Cover and shake well then store in a cool place for at least a month. Shake the jar at least once a week. When you are ready to serve, strain through a colander and a cloth into a decanter. Makes about 4 ½ cups.

Mint Julep

(All ingredients are measured to preference)
bourbon
shaved ice
mint leaves
sugar

Chill some tall, thin glasses. Place a sprig of mint, teaspoon of sugar and a teaspoon of bourbon into each glass. Mash the ingredients together. Fill each glass to the brim with ice, then fill with bourbon. Stir well and garnish with a sprig of mint.

Newfoundland Blueberry Wine

9 $1/2$ cups blueberries
19 cups boiling water
6 cups granulated sugar
3 cups prunes

Place blueberries and boiling water in a large kettle. Bring to a boil. Strain and measure. For each gallon (20 cups) juice, stir in 6 cups granulated sugar. Boil for 5 minutes. Cool and add 3 cups prunes. Place in crock or jar. Cover with cheesecloth and let stand for 2 months. Strain, bottle and cork.

Dandelion Wine

20 cups boiling water
14 $1/2$ cups dandelion blooms
juice of 3 lemons
juice of 1 orange
3 pounds granulated sugar
1 slice toast
$1/2$ yeast cake

Pour boiling water over 14 $1/2$ cups of dandelion blooms. Let stand overnight. Strain. Stir into liquid the lemon juice, orange juice and sugar. Boil for 30 minutes. Cool. Spread the toast with the yeast cake and add to the liquid. Let stand for 4 weeks, or until fermentation ceases. Bottle and cork well.

Red Velvet Punch

8 cups cranberry cocktail
1 can frozen orange juice
1 can frozen pineapple juice
1 can frozen lemonade
2 (750 ml) bottles ginger ale
1 litre bottle white grape juice

Mix together in punch bowl. Top with lime and lemon slices. Makes 20 to 25 servings.

Dandelion Coffee

To enjoy the entire plant, reserve the roots of the dandelion and clean them well, but do not remove their brown skin. Cut them into bean size pieces and roast on a baking sheet in the oven until they are brown and crisp like coffee beans. Grind and prepare like normal coffee for a mellow cup of java.

Megan Follows and Jonathon Cronbie in "Anne of Green Gables - The Continuing Story"

Preserves

A community picnic was the height of social activity in Avonlea, complete with cakes and delicious preserves such as strawberry jams, potted shrimps, pickled pears and candied tomatoes. Anne forever treasured the day when she attended her first picnic with Marilla over on Orchard Slope. It was the first time she tasted ice cream, which she described as "sublime" and it was where she made her first bosom friend, Diana Barry.

Peach Marmalade

3 oranges
1 cup water
12 large peaches
6 cups granulated sugar

Cut the oranges in half then slice very thinly. Place the oranges in a saucepan and simmer for 15 minutes to soften the skins. Stone the peaches leaving the skins on and slice. Measure the quantity of jars by packing the pieces tightly into cups. Add 1 cup of sugar to each cup of peaches before stirring into the simmering oranges. Boil for about 20 minutes. Pour the marmalade into sterilized jars and cover with melted wax. Makes 10 to 16 cups.

Black Cherry & Red Currant Jam

3 cups red currant juice
5 cups pitted black cherries
6 ¾ cups granulated sugar
¼ teaspoon salt
½ teaspoon almond extract

Combine the red currant juice and black cherries in a large pot. Bring to a boil and simmer until the cherries are soft. Add the sugar and boil vigorously until the liquid begins to gel (about 30 minutes) stirring the entire time. Add salt and extract and bottle in hot sterilized jars. Store in a cool place. Makes 8 cups.

Blueberry Jam

6 cups blueberries, washed and stemmed
2 tablespoons lemon juice
1 tablespoon grated lemon rind
¼ teaspoon cinnamon
2 cups granulated sugar

Combine all ingredients into a large saucepan or kettle. Boil for 5 minutes or until desired consistency (when cool) is achieved. Ladle into sterilized jars and seal. Makes ten 6-ounce jars.

Sunshine Strawberry Jam

4 cups fresh strawberries, stemmed and hulled
4 cups granulated sugar
2 tablespoons lemon juice

Boil ingredients together, uncovered, for 8-10 minutes. Stir frequently. Pour into shallow containers and cover with plastic wrap. Prop to allow evaporation. Set in sun, stirring occasionally, until desired thickness. Berries should be suspended whole in the jelly, which may take 2-3 days. Place into sterilized jars and seal. Makes six 6-ounce jars.

Spiced Crabapple Jelly

29 cups (6 quarts) crabapples
5 1/4 cups crabapple juice
1/2 cup white vinegar
1 (4-inch) Cinnamon stick (broken)
1 tablespoon whole Cloves
5 cups granulated sugar

Wash and remove blossom ends and stems from crabapples. Combine in a large saucepan with enough water to cover. Bring to a boil and simmer, uncovered, for 20 minutes, or until mushy. Strain through jelly bag overnight. In a saucepan, combine crabapple juice with white vinegar. Tie in cheesecloth and add cinnamon stick and cloves. Bring to a boil and leave uncovered for 3 minutes. Remove spice bag. Stir in granulated sugar slowly. Allow cooling and setting overnight.

Wine Jelly

2 cups favorite wine
2 1/2 cups granulated sugar
1/2 bottle Certo

Measure wine and sugar into top of double boiler. Mix well. Place over rapidly boiling water and heat 4 minutes, stirring constantly. Remove from water and at once stir in Certo. Pour quickly into glasses. Makes five 8 oz. glasses. Use Port Wine for steaks, roasts and chops, or White Wine for fish, poultry and eggs. Sherry Wine may be served with any main course dish.

Green Tomato & Green Apple Chutney

3 cups chopped green tomatoes
2 tablespoons coarse salt
4 cups white vinegar
2 tablespoons salt
4 cups brown sugar
6 cups chopped, unripened, peeled green apples
1 cup chopped onion
3 cups seedless raisins
1/4 cup peeled and chopped ginger root
2 tablespoons mustard seed
2 tablespoons all-purpose flour
1/4 cup cold water

Sprinkle the tomatoes with coarse salt and allow to stand for 12 hours then drain. Combine the vinegar, salt and brown sugar in a large pot. Add the apples, onions, tomatoes, raisins, ginger and mustard seed and cook gently, stirring, until soft (about 45 minutes). Combine flour and cold water and add to chutney. Cook for 5 minutes. Bottle in sterilized jars and allow to stand for 6 weeks prior to serving.

Chili Sauce

30 tomatoes
6 large onions, thinly sliced
4 red peppers, finely chopped
2 hot peppers, seeded and finely chopped
1 cup cider vinegar
2 tablespoons coarse salt
2 cups granulated sugar
1/2 cup mixed pickling spice, wrapped in a cheesecloth bag

Peel and chop the tomatoes and heat them in a large saucepan until they are softened. Strain off about 4 cups of the juice then add in the remaining ingredients. Stir gently for about 2 hours or until desired thickness is achieved. Remove the pickling spice and bottle sauce in sterile jars and seal.

Corn Relish

1 tablespoon cornstarch
¼ cup water
one (12 oz) can of corn, undrained
⅓ cup granulated sugar
⅓ cup white vinegar
1 teaspoon turmeric
1 green onion, finely chopped
½ teaspoon celery seed

Blend the cornstarch and water into a paste in a small saucepan. Add the other ingredients and mix well. Cook the mixture over medium heat, while stirring. The mixture will thicken just before the boiling point. Remove from the heat and allow to cool before placing the relish into small jars. Store in the refrigerator. Makes about 2 cups.

Rhubarb Relish

8 cups fresh rhubarb, cut into ½ inch pieces
1 cup chopped onions
1 cup white vinegar
2 ½ cups granulated sugar
½ teaspoon ground ginger
1 teaspoon cinnamon
½ teaspoon ground cloves
1 tablespoon pickling salt

Combine all of the ingredients into a large saucepan. Bring to a boil and allow to simmer until thickened (about 45 minutes). Stir frequently until the consistency of applesauce is attained. Remove from heat and allow to cool before putting in sterilized jars and sealing. Makes 6 cups

Bread & Butter Pickles

16 cups cubed cucumbers, preferably small
6 large white onions, sliced
3 cloves garlic
1 large green pepper
1 large red pepper
⅓ cup pickling (coarse) salt
3 cups white vinegar

5 cups brown sugar
1 ½ teaspoons turmeric
1 ½ teaspoons celery seeds
2 tablespoons mustard seeds

Cube cucumbers and add garlic, onions, green and red peppers (in strips) together. Add salt. Mix well. In a very large pot, place this mixture and cover with ice cubes. Let stand at least three hours. Drain well. Boil sugar and vinegar. In a small linen cloth, put the turmeric, celery seeds and mustard seeds and tie at the top. Also boil this little white bag with the sugar and vinegar until it comes to a rolling boil. Into this hot mixture, put the cucumber mixture. Bring the whole thing to a boil. Discard the white bag. Place into hot sterilized jars, making sure that the edges of the jars are not sticky or wet. Seal in the usual manner, making certain that the top lid is very hot (having been sterilized) and dry and tighten immediately. Turn the jars upside-down overnight and then store.

Mustard Pickles

2 heads cauliflower
9 ½ cups small cucumbers
9 ½ cups Silverskin onions
4 ¾ cups yellow string beans
2 green peppers
7 cups vinegar
¼ pound dry mustard
3 teaspoons turmeric
1 teaspoon celery seed
3-4 cups brown sugar
1 cup flour

Cut vegetables in small pieces, cover with boiling brine and let stand overnight. Wash with cold water and drain well. Mix mustard, flour, sugar and enough vinegar to make a smooth paste. Add remaining vinegar and cook until mixture thickens. Add all the vegetables and cook 20 minutes, stirring continuously. Seal in sterile jars.

Pickled Mushrooms

⅓ cup dry white wine
⅓ cup white wine vinegar
⅓ cup vegetable oil
1 small onion, thinly sliced
2 tablespoons chopped parsley
1 clove garlic, chopped
1 bay leaf
1 teaspoon salt
¼ teaspoon dried thyme
a pinch of pepper
1 pound fresh mushrooms

Combine all of the ingredients except for the mushrooms in a saucepan and bring to a boil. Add the mushrooms and return to a boil. Simmer, uncovered, for 10 minutes. Chill in an uncovered container for a day. Will keep for 2 weeks if stored in the refrigerator.

Pickled Herring

6 salt herring
3 large onions
2 ½ cups white vinegar
2 tablespoons pickling spice
½ cup granulated sugar
6 Bay leaves

Allow the herring to sit in water over night. Rinse and squeeze out excess water. Cut off the heads and tails and remove the skin. Fillet the fish and cut into bit size pieces. Slice the onions and place into sterilized jars, alternating layers of onion and herring. Heat the vinegar to the boiling point in a saucepan then add the pickling spice and sugar and allow to simmer for 10 minutes. Let the liquid cool, then strain it over the herring. Place a bay leaf in each jar and store in the refrigerator. Ready to serve after two days, this appetizer or salad topper should keep for several weeks. Makes up to 6 jars.

Pickled Eggs

12 hard boiled eggs
1 cup canned beet juice
1 cup cider vinegar
1 clove garlic
1 bay leaf
1 teaspoon salt
1/4 teaspoon pepper

While peeling the eggs, bring the other ingredients to a boil in a small saucepan. Put the eggs in a large glass jar and pour over the juice. Allow eggs to cool for a few days before serving. Store in the refrigerator; will keep for at least two months.

Megan Follows and Colleen Dewhurst in "Anne of Green Gables"

Victorian Parlour Games

After enjoying a fine dinner, long before the dawn of television and DVD players, Anne and her guests would likely have retired to the parlor room for some relaxing and entertaining parlor games. Here are a few of the traditional games that you may enjoy with your guests.

THE ADVERB GAME

Guests are divided into two teams and a Guesser from each team is sent out of the room. While they are gone the rest of the guests decide on an adverb like "rapidly". When the Guessers return they must try to uncover the secret word by asking each guest in turn questions like "Do you like my sweater?". The answer must be given in a manner corresponding with the secret adverb. The first Guesser to correctly identify the adverb gains a point for their team.

ALLITERATION ALPHABET

This is a popular game that has many variations of play. The first method is to have the guests try to carry on a normal conversation by each saying a sentence that has a minimum of five-words. The key though is their sentence must be a complete alliteration and must be of the next letter of the alphabet. For example, Emily could successfully begin by saying, "Anne absolutely adored Averil's Atonement." Then Felicity would continue by declaring, "But bits bored the Barrys". Felicity would get one strike for not using at least 5 words. Fred would continue alphabetically by stating, "The Barry clan complained of cloying, complicated communique." Fred gets one strike for using "Barry" since it does not begin with the letter 'C'. When a player gets three strikes they are out of the game and the winner is the last player remaining.

QUESTIONS?

In this game the guests try to hold a normal conversation but every sentence must be in the form of a question. When someone fails to phrase their words as an interrogation they are out of the game. The winner is the last person remaining.

Richard Farnsworth and Colleen Dewhurst in "Anne of Green Gables"

CHOCOLATE WAR

Always a favorite among ladies, the object of the game is to eat as much chocolate as possible. Each player takes turns rolling a die. If they roll a six they have a chance to eat some delicious chocolate. The catch, however, is that they must first put on a cumbersome costume such as a pair of snow pants, scarf, hat, mittens, coat and galoshes before they can eat the chocolate using a knife and fork. (It would be perfect to have a period costume to dress up in, complete with petticoat and pinafore instead of snowgear!) While the potential chocolate eater is doing this, the other players are rolling the die. When someone else rolls a six the pursuer must stop and the next person tries. Play continues until all the chocolate has been devoured.

QUOTABLE QUOTES

This is a game for connoisseurs of literature. Begin by selecting a passage from one of your favorite authors like Lucy Maud Montgomery. Read the beginning and end of the quotation, omitting 1 or 2 sentences in the middle. The guests are then instructed to fill in the gap with their best prose. The attempts are collected and read aloud along with the correct quotation. Guests vote on which prose they think is the correct answer. They may also vote for the most entertaining entry.

VERY PUNNY

This is a hilarious play on words game. A subject is chosen such as Animals and then each guest takes a turn in creating a pun. Play continues until no more puns can be made.

"Don't you go lion to me again, it would break my heart."
"This is delicious chocolate moose!"

MEMORY GAME

A simple and classic game that is very challenging. To play, one person is selected to be The Guesser. They observe a room or a box filled with knick-knacks and are given 30 seconds to memorize their subject. Then they are sent out of the room. The remaining guests make subtle changes to the room or knick-knacks such as hiding a cushion, adding/removing a knick-knack, etc. The Guesser is then brought back in and tries to notice as many changes as possible.

Megan Follows in "Anne of Green Gables"

NOTES

NOTES